THE
FLAMING
SWORD

FOLAYAN OSEKITA

Trafford
PUBLISHING™

ISBN: 978-1-4251-2156-3 (sc)
ISBN: 978-1-4269-3366-0 (dj)
ISBN: 978-1-4269-3323-3 (eb)

*Our mission is to efficiently provide the world's finest, most comprehensive
book publishing service, enabling every author to experience success.
To find out how to publish your book, your way, and have it available
worldwide, visit us online at www.trafford.com*

Traffor rev 04/30/2010

Trafford
PUBLISHING™   www.trafford.com

North America & international
toll-free: 1 888 232 4444 (USA & Canada)
phone: 250 383 6864 ♦ fax: 812 355 4082 ♦ email: info@trafford.com

Contents

Extracts from the Word of God

Genesis 3:24

After he drove the man out, he placed on the east side of the Garden of Eden cherubim and a **Flaming Sword** flashing back and forth to guard the way to the tree of life.

Ephesians 6:17

Take the helmet of salvation and the **Sword** of the **Spirit**, which is the word of God.

Hebrews 4:12

For the word of God is living and active. **Sharper than any double-edged sword**, it penetrates even to dividing soul and spirit, joints and marrow; it judges the thoughts and attitudes of the heart.

The Flaming Sword is the Sword of the Spirit, which is the Word of God. The Word of God is Living and Active. Jesus Christ is the Word of God. He is Living and is Active. He is the Living God.

For, in the beginning was the Word and the Word was with God and the Word was God. He was with God in the beginning. (John 1:1-2).

Praise and Dedication

To God be the Glory; for, great things He Has Done. So loved He the world, that He gave us His Son (Jesus Christ), who yielded His Life unto death, to atone for sin. For this reason alone it is worthy for all creation to praise the Lord. Let everything that has breath praise the Lord. Halleluyah! Amen. Thank You Jesus. Halleluyah!

Who is like You O God? How Excellent You are. In all of Heaven and earth, who is like You? There is no one. There is nobody like You O Lord, God. Amen. You Are the Holy One of Israel. When You Build, no one can destroy what You Build. When You Open, no one can shut what You Open. Likewise, when You choose to destroy, no one can rebuild again. As the trees abound and the plants spread, not a leaf shall fall to the ground, except at Your Command, and by Your Will.

How could I thank You for Your manifold and plentifully abundant Grace, Mercy and Love unto me and my household with me? With what shall I express and or give my thanks, to show the depth of my appreciation and gratitude? You have done great and mighty things in my life, too many to recount. That I live today even to deliver this short message to this world as we know it, is solely by Your Power; nothing to do with me or my wisdom and or ability.

That You Grant me this opportunity to testify and witness to how Worthy You Are, and how Great and Mighty beyond any human questioning and or comprehension, I am truly Divinely Blessed and Highly Favoured. That You would take a worthless thing like me, of the dust of the earth and absolutely the worst of all sinners, undeserving of any goodness whatsoever from a Holy God as You Truly Are; and make me into a useful vessel is beyond my imagination O God.

To transform me as You Have into an instrument through which You Choose to speak to the world – a watchman, an oracle, a prophet, an evangelist and apostle of our Lord Jesus Christ; even a witness in these last days to the unchanging, yet ever dynamic in manifestation (ever changing) nature of God through Jesus Christ – the same yesterday, today and forevermore – is an overwhelming experience and most humbling O Lord.

I stand and live in awe of You. I am absolutely terrified with the depth of Your Love for me. The world must hear and know by my own hand and mouth that You have chosen me out of nothing.

I can no longer keep this Great Joy, this overwhelming Light of Your Love to myself, my household, and the many individuals that You have Sent to me and vice-versa alone. I must speak out.

This Word is too hot within me and will destroy me if shut in. Unless I preach the Word, I am doomed. I faintly grasp the words of Paul the Apostle who said woe unto him if he did not preach the Gospel. O Lord my God, how Great You truly are.

This Great Testimony must flow through me O Lord, lest I perish. Woe unto me if I do not do Your Will to the very end – to declare with Your authority that You my God Are Holy, Awesome and Greatly to be feared, worshipped, praised and adored. We are created to fear God and to obey His Commandments.

We are fearfully made, we are wonderfully made, we belong to God; we resemble Him. That is why the devil trembles whenever he hears us singing praises unto God thankfully and fearfully. We are God's own. We are the apples of His Eyes when we fear Him and obey His Commandments – the evidence of our love for Him.

O Lord God Almighty, kindly accept and Bless this my first fruits (to the world at large) – in terms of written declaration of Your Counsel to me over these many years of sojourn on earth and in particular in London, England in the United Kingdom. All the way from my little and great university (University Of Ado-Ekiti) village of Iworoko-Ekiti, Ekiti State, Nigeria, West Africa, Africa.

You O Lord have been my Helper, my Rock, a veritable Help in times of trouble (and there have been many). Through so many diverse travails – of racial hatred and other forms of discrimination (so severe); long term unemployment, sickness, near loss of marriage and life. You have kept me safely thus far. You are Good.

Faced with persistent hatred and opposition, discouragement, untold hardships, beatings, incarceration in police cells with threats of more, threats to my life (including with a hammer and guns) and family; and most gruesomely painful of all, threats from the powers that be to put me in jail in order to prevent me from family worship unto You my God and much more.

I rejoice today in Your Awesome Assurance of Victory in all that I face in life; for my Lord Jesus Christ overcame this world. In spite of all, Your Love Prevails firmly over my life. You have continued to sustain my family (regardless of much brokenness in body and of spirit). Your allowing me (us) to be broken has Blessed us with contrition in our hearts. We live to witness to the fact that You, O Lord our God, Are Faithful, and ever so sure.

You Are Kind, Loving, Holy, All-Consuming Fire, Worthy and You Are God. Jesus Christ is Your Name (above all names). The only Name (Jesus) Given unto mankind, by and through which all may come and access Your Holy Throne of Mercy and Grace.

Jesus Christ, who died and Rose again after three days is Your One and Only Son, Seeded of Your Holy Spirit and not flesh. Jesus Christ is now Seated a the Right Side of Your Glorious Presence, on Your Holy and Most Powerful and Resplendent Throne forever and ever. Amen. Forever and ever, Jesus Christ is Lord, over all of Heaven and earth, both now and forevermore. Amen.

Soon to come is this Jesus Christ, to Judge the world and take His Own with Him to Rule and Reign and be with Him over the New Jerusalem from Heaven, where the Holy Ones dwell. Jerusalem, the City of God, where there shall be no more sorrow, pain, tears, fear, etc., only Praises, Joy in Light and no darkness. Jerusalem, the City of God with Pearly Gates and Pure Gold Paved Streets.

O how I long for Thee O Lord Jesus and for Your Holy City, Jerusalem; to be with Thee O Lord Jesus Christ with Your Holy Ones in the Great City to come, the City of our God. Amen. It is unto You O Father, in Jesus Christ's Holy Name (with much fear and trembling) that I give and declare my thanks and praises and adoration at this time, for giving me this Blessed opportunity to reach out through the vehicle You Spoke unto me in the ministry of Windows Of Heaven, a Revival Outreach.

Windows of Heaven Revival Outreach, for the salvation of those whom You have Decided before hand in Your Mercy; and for a sign, an encouragement unto God's beloved, scattered around the world. It is unto You that I dedicate this message (book), to usher in a new era, by Your Word, in Jesus' Holy Name. Amen. Father, may my witness manifest Your Glory in Jesus' Name. Amen.

Thank You Father; Thank You Son; Thank You Holy Spirit. Accept my gratitude Father, in Jesus' Name I pray Thee, Amen. Now, Father God, Son of God, Holy Spirit of God, as You always do, once again, Send Forth Your Word With Power to spread across the nations of the world as You have Promised. Prove Yourself Holy in my life and service unto You in this service to which You Called me unto my fellow human beings.

Lord, I thank You, for I know that You always Answer me and Will Prove that You Lord Have Sent me; and my family (household) with me, in Jesus' Name, Amen.

I honour You O Lord with my everything; and with my all, my household inclusive, I dedicate these live oracles to You O Lord my God and King, Jesus Christ is Your Name. Amen. May the oracles, these words that You have Inspired me to write, the words of my mouth and the meditations in my heart, always be acceptable in Your Glorious Sight and Presence, in Jesus' Name, I pray. Amen.

In this endeavour, I am representing to You, O Lord, that which You Blessed me with, as a beginning, the first-fruits, in the hope of more to come. In Jesus' Name, Father, for Jesus' Name's sake, accept my thanksgiving and dedication this day. Amen.

Acknowledgements...

I want to thank God for the lives of Mr and Dr (Mrs) Tunde Sokan; Mr Olatoye Oladeji; Mr and Mrs Dupe Omotoso; Dr Gbenga Sangowawa; Rev Ademola Aladejana; Dianne Howard; Fran Gero and Denise Watts for their continued support and encouragement. A special thanks to Kent Uche, CEO, Naija FM (www.naijafm. com), who gave me a platform to further propagate the Gospel of Jesus Christ and Mayowa Rufai, for his help with the book cover. I must acknowledge and thank Mr and Mrs Michael Lawson, for a very frank, painstaking and thorough critique of the first draft of this book. For my family – my wife, Temitope, our sons, Folayo, Debodun and Misimi, Lord, I thank You especially, for they have made this effort and ministry a bearable joy, not a burden. Thank you and I love you all.

Note to the Reader

Prayerfully consider the following extracts from Michael Lawson's comments:

"... There are a few of the points that you have made that I would not have thought of, but then again that is what a prophet is for – to tell people about things that God needs them to know but they would not have thought of... "

"... I have tried to detach myself from my own views and think of how a wide range of readers may respond. I have also tried to think of the prophesy as having come from an anonymous source, so that I am commenting on it and not on you... "

"... There are people who may be put off reading because of the introduction, who should read it and may benefit from doing so. It may be interpreted in a perverse way and you could be unfairly blamed for the consequences of the readers' foolishness... "

"... Finally, I would like to say that I believe that what you have written needs to be published so that it can be considered seriously by as many people as possible, both inside and outside the Church. I would very much like it to be a focus of prayer and discussion in the Church. It is most important that those who are in the Church learn to look at what they are doing from a different perspective, and see themselves in a different light. Let us hope and pray that it may be so."

I must say that Michael's final thoughts aptly convey the essence of the message in driving home the need for urgent reflection. More importantly, the penultimate paragraph's potential challenge to persevere and not be put off at all by anything read in the introductory stages of the book. May God Guide you all my readers as you progress right through to the very end. I pray in Jesus' Name. Amen.

It would be a great help to all to take this challenging frankness and thoughtfulness into consideration and if possible come back to it at any stage where personal or other sentiments may temporarily be in the way. This will ensure that all readers get the most out of these words as the Lord Gave unto me. The Ultimate Judge of course is God. Whilst the Word of God clearly tells us not to judge, lest we be judged (Luke 6:37). However, we are also told that the man of God will be a judge of all things but be subject to no man's judgment (1 Corinthians 2:14-16). Paul reminds us of this too (1 Corinthians 4:3-4).

May God Enrich you fully as you receive His Word as delivered by His servant. Amen.

I strongly urge and challenge you, my reader, to humble yourself and open your mind totally; to painstakingly read this message as a child would in an attitude of respect, meditation and as in praying (even if u never did/do) to a Holy, Loving, Awesome God.

In so doing, you will come to taste (for sure) God's Love (even if you have never done so before) in a new light. His Truth and His Word too will become likewise unto all who will diligently hearken unto this short counsel in your approach to this message (book).

You will begin to find out for yourself (perhaps for the first time) that God in Jesus Christ is forever and altogether Good and Gracious and Merciful. Also, that God is Able to Forgive you through Jesus Christ, His Son.

You will begin to know in a deep, pure, and holy spiritual sense that in Truth, only in Jesus Christ can you find true freedom that we all seek (and or sought after), before we come into this Gracious Truth in Jesus Christ. This truth is in Jesus Christ alone and only this Truth can set anyone free. Be fully assured of this fact, that whomsoever the Son of God (Jesus Christ) sets free is free indeed.

So, I challenge you, dare you, urge you, and encourage you passionately, with my whole being to relax fully in your mind, soul, heart, body and all. Let your total being be at peace with your Creator and be free from the cares of life (anxieties, worries, fears etc., the whole lot). Let the peace of God the Creator be with you.

Unburden yourself of all trepidation, and for now, cast all cares unto Jesus Christ, who already paid the price – by His death on the Cross at Calvary, for all who will come to Him and trust and believe in His Supreme Sacrifice.

That is to say that whether you like it or not; knew it or not; Jesus Christ loves you with great potential; and showed this love in dying for you too, and not just for those who proclaim His Name as Lord and Saviour. By this, you too have an opportunity to come to God through faith in Jesus Christ to become born again, and earn your right to become a child of God.

Whether you understand these words or not, at this time, do not fret or be agitated or even angry or upset. The devil will not want you to soak in this message; so determine within yourself that nothing will cause you to miss this Word from God to you in Jesus' Name. Amen.

Be very patient, penitent, focused, willing and totally ready to receive (supernaturally) pardon and direction for the future. Let it not surprise you that my Lord Will Reveal Himself to you (some for the first time ever) in the course of soaking in this message.

The Word of God is Timeless and is for all time. God, my God, in Jesus' Christ, Will Grant you Divine Favour as you obey sincerely.

When you read this message with the mindset of a child – as I encouraged and urged you to – you will never be the same again.

My God in Jesus Christ Will open your ears, hearts, and minds to hear, understand and know deeply that this Word is for you and that God's Word is sharper than any double edged sword, able to separate even bone from marrow. The Word of God Will come Alive for you in Jesus' Name as you obey.

So, in advance, I say to you – may my God through Jesus Christ Bless you and honour your obedience in Jesus' Name I pray thankfully. Amen. Be prepared therefore.

Somebody is going to be Blessed with this Message. Someone will be set free from bondage(s). Someone will receive the Holy Spirit. Someone will be healed. Someone will be broken. Someone will be rebuilt. Someone will be shaken up thoroughly from soaking in this message and putting God's Word to good use. Be delivered in Jesus' Name. Amen.

Someone will begin to enter into maturity in the Faith. Someone will come into the Faith. There is a Holy Anointing that will follow the faithful and the Holy Spirit will be Sent to them who choose to be faithful in Jesus' Name. Receive yours now in Jesus' Name. Amen.

Some renewing of minds will take place. Some retarded people in every sense of the word will come alive and begin to grow normally; right now in Jesus' Name, come alive. Amen.

Some will be healed miraculously; some over time and some instantly – all according to your faith. Believe and do not doubt. Again, the Lord has Spoken. Be fully humble and receive blessings, miracles, healings, wisdom, etc. from Jesus Christ and in Jesus' Name. Amen.

You wonder why? Jesus Christ spoke a long time ago through the Prophets that He Sent His Word and Healed Your infirmities.

There is Great and Mighty Power in the Word of God. Just believe.

I bid you Peace in Jesus' Name. For your obedience, by faith I say to you, CONGRATULATIONS, as you receive True Freedom in Jesus Christ. Amen.

A CASE FOR THE WORD OF GOD:
Gateway to True Freedom

I was Blessed to acquire the biggest Holy Bible I have ever seen and touched to date: "Imperial Family Bible". I was simply awestruck.

The Lord Spoke to me a long time ago, that I should seek after His Word earnestly. He Began to Teach me Himself through diverse means and revelations on a daily basis (especially in the last twelve to twenty-one years) and with intense love and passion.

I had not realised that, all my life, I had been going through the preparation for God's Word to me. God is indeed Holy and Awesome.

As I studied the Introduction (Section III), I was suddenly moved very deeply with regard to how devoted some men were, to the task of translating the Word of God (Old and New Testament Holy Scriptures) into the language understandable by common ordinary people of other nations, apart from the original Hebrew, Aramaic and Greek languages, in which the Scriptures were either received directly or translated, especially in the earlier times.

Monks had spent time devoted to translation; and painstakingly copying the Holy Scriptures by hand, in order to preserve them in the best possible, most beautiful way, for posterity.

This arduous task could only have been Ordained by God and only God could have Given those workers the inspiration, passion and zeal on a daily basis to carry out the task faithfully and to the best of their ability.

We enjoy the labour of such workers today and it is easy to take their work for granted. I bow to God in Christ Jesus in honour of our God in the lives of these workers and the likes of them. God be praised forevermore in Christ Jesus, Amen.

I therefore submit that, it is a great Blessing for anyone to be a "custodian" of the Word of God. That is saying, to be a watchman over God's flocks. This is a great privilege which none must ever abuse. To abuse this great charge is to incur the wrath of God.

It is the fear of God and the awe resulting from this that draws certain people to the Word of God and makes them so boldly determined to fulfil whatever inspired strong desire is rooted deep within them by this great God, from whom the Word of God emanates, flows, laden with such Power.

God speaks forth as He Wills, even today, regardless of the intrigues of mankind. I am the Lord and I do not change. God is forevermore. Do not let your mind and heart lead you astray. Receive Jesus Christ into your life today. You must be born again to know the true life that pleases God.

Of Judgements...

Augustin (St Austin), a Roman monk (1st Archbishop of Canterbury) was sent by Gregory I with 40 others to convert the inhabitants of Great Britain. Painstaking efforts were made to replicate the Word of God in the local language of many peoples, including Anglo-Saxons (also English) – a most arduous task.

Generally, although there is great appreciation for this work and research continues to support the fact that there is no book that sells in the world like the Holy Bible, over many years past, to date, many malign the Word and claim that there is too much inconsistency etc. However, from available evidence, surely, God is With His Word and Watches over His Word to fulfil His Word and His Word Stands Forevermore. Amen.

Jeremiah the Prophet wrote of God gracefully, that the lying pens of the Scribes have handled the Word of God falsely (Jeremiah 8:8). This was no deliberate effort of man solely, but a device of satanic intent and cunning.

We can liken this to the "enemy having sown tares" secretly, amongst the true believers in the Word of God. These "words" are attributed to Jesus Christ Himself in the Holy Scriptures' New Testament. Humans need God's Holy Spirit therefore, to decipher God's Word.

Jesus Christ likened the Kingdom of God to a farmland cultivated by a farmer for wheat; but the enemy secretly sowed tares amongst the wheat. However, in the fullness of time, all will be revealed for what is sown – whether tares or wheat – the former will be gathered as will the latter. One to be harvested for good use (the wheat) and the other for burning and destruction (the tares).

Therefore, for anyone to be truly inclined towards and drawn to believe the Word of God, the test must be love. Love begets a sure, faithful devotion and obedience to the object of love, with the desire to please. When you love someone, you do not want to offend them, excepting for building them up for good not for ill. It is almost like you fear that making that person you love sad for no good reason will cause their potential to love you to reduce, albeit not necessarily so.

Here, I speak of the Love of and for the Word of God, which is very excellently unravelled in the Holy Scriptures' New Testament Book of 1 Corinthians 13. This applies even as the Word of God instructs and explains for us to test all spirits to see if they are from God. Love is testable and continuously so.

The taste of the pudding they say is in the eating of it (and not in the making, I add). The taste of love is in the actual loving and not in the promise, saying, feigning of it etc. Love is an action, a decision. Love cannot be forced. It flows from within, freely, potentially prone to, and ultimately overcoming all inhibition.

Love is for real. Love is not what you think, feel, taste, smell, touch, see, take and drop. Love is Spiritual. Love is Holy, Pure and Secure. Love is quite shakeable, but indestructible. Love's Roots are Firm. Hence, love overcomes all things in the long haul.

The Bible says the only thing that matters is faith that works through love (Galatians 5:6). Love never loses hope, but hopes all things; love always perseveres and will not give up; love always believes; love always trusts; love surely is supreme and never fails. God is Love (1 John 4:8) and Love is God.

God is the Ultimate Judge. Jesus Christ is His Name. The only Name Given unto mankind through which we may be saved (Acts 12:4) is the Name of Jesus. At the Name of Jesus, every knee shall bow and every tongue shall confess that Jesus Christ is Lord (Isaiah 45:23; Philippians 2:10-12); and that is why you who know that you are in Christ Jesus as in having been saved, born again, must work out your salvation with fear and trembling. Who is the Lord except our God? (2 Samuel 22:32; Psalm 18:31) Amen.

The bottom line is to fear God and obey His Commandments (Ecclesiastes 12:13).

Of Faith…

When you love someone, you just believe in the person; you trust the person (in love) with all your heart and when they make you a promise, like a child, you just trust that they will fulfil that promise. Love believes all things truly. Remember Jesus said no one can enter the Kingdom of God except they accept it as a little child (Matthew 18:2-3).

Although love may repeatedly be disappointed, love is never disappointing. Love keeps on. This is why before anyone can truly believe in the Word of God, one must fully and absolutely fall for the Word of God in love. It just happens. Many look for this experience in vain. Some wait in vain likewise. God Blesses whomsoever He Chooses to Bless.

Some find this strange and rather hypocritical and call believers names until they come to know what the believers know. I am most guilty of having done this. Truly, there must be some sense in the saying that there is a joy in being mad which none but the mad ones know.

Faith comes by hearing; hearing by the Word of the Lord. How can anyone hear unless preached to? Can anyone believe a God they do not know or see and never heard of? Again, how can anyone preach unless sent? (Romans 10:14-17) But I am on the matter of faith for now.

Like I mentioned earlier, with love somehow comes a fear – not an unholy fear but an awesome, reverent, respectful fear – that draws together the lover and the loved. One must be in awe of the Author of the Word of God to be able to demonstrably love Him and not just say one wants to come to God but to come to God and learn

His Ways and put them to practice and be obedient. This pleases God and then a relationship is struck with great potential to grow.

Even as the Holy Scriptures hold that faith comes through hearing the Word of God; the Scriptures go further to ask how anyone can believe in a God that they do not know? How can they know God unless they are preached to? How can they (who preach to them) do so – unless they are Sent to preach etc. God Sends, not man.

The Word of God is indeed amazing to behold and only by deep, ongoing, constant studying, meditation upon, application (putting into constant use is a must), sharing, teaching, learning witnessing, testifying, etc. can anyone truly faithfully adhere to the Word of God. Any true follower shall bear much fruit, fruits that last. The true follower of Jesus Christ shall remain fruitful as long as such remain in Him and He in them (John 15:1-8).

The Holy Scriptures encourage us deeply to teach our children so they can teach their children, who in turn can teach their children etc. (Deuteronomy 4:9-11; 11:9-11; 11:19) when we have learnt the Word of God and His Ways. We must share with posterity via this enduring spiritual strategy. To obey of course is better than sacrifice (1 Samuel 15:22). To learn the Word of God, we must submit to the Almighty God, to the Authority of the Word of God (God Himself).

When we truly hallow the Word of God as Authored by Him, He (God) Will Honour His Promise to Reveal unto us great and manifold Treasures of Love, Righteousness, Peace, Joy etc. which otherwise remain hidden from the unbelieving and disobedient. We must realise that obedience is a sure reflection of true love as spoken by Jesus Christ Himself. If you love me, you will obey my Commandments, Jesus said (John 14:21-24).

Obedience is a sure test of anyone's true love for God and for the Word of God (Jesus Christ). Jesus made very clear that if you love Him, you will obey His Commandments. Obedience cannot be overemphasized. Obedience is key to walking with God. Trust and obey; no other way. Only faith can please God in any of mankind.

Without faith no one can please God (Hebrews 11:6). So, if you want to please God, you must have faith in His Word. Believe Him. Abraham believed God and it was counted unto Him as righteousness. It is faith that enables true love to flow even unto faithful obedience.

When combined with attending willing, wilful submission, faith is made strong unto love and unto accepting the Authority of the Word of God. I remember the song trust and obey for there is no other way, to be joyful in Jesus is to trust and obey.

Faith is what enables us to believe and obey without a doubt-led disposition to argue, contest, dishonour, question and disobey the Word of God; and or make flimsy excuses for not obeying the Word of God and His Commandments and Instructions.

Some make excuses like the Word was not meant for this generation; we must move with the times; God never meant it that way; God is love (yes, but His Word must be obeyed); well, we are all at different levels, don't judge me, it's by Grace, etc.

No, such people lack love and are devoid of the true faith-driven obedience of spirit, which invokes the Enabling Holy Spirit of God onto and upon the true believer(s) for the ability to live a Godly life in Jesus Christ. Such people are false and are very well endowed to move swiftly to propagate their teaching, which spreads like gangrene. The Bible warns against such falsehoods. They are false prophets.

False prophets love to deceive and give people a false sense of security and salvation; they come in sheep's clothing but are ferocious wolves. They will perform great signs and miracles to deceive the elect – if that were possible. (Matthew 7:15; 24:10-12,

24). In fact they will make you feel good and tell you all is well with you and speak well of you as the people did to the false prophets (Luke 6:26). The feel good factor is one of their prime strategies.

The Word of God is not divided and is not subject to our manipulation. There is grave danger for anyone who adds to or takes from the Word of God (Revelation 22:18-19). This is eternal damnation and definite exemption from the Life. So, all who believe must be very careful not to be led astray in these last days.

If anyone says they cannot be led astray and or deceived, then they are already lost. The devil (satan) is very crafty and will use any means to lead many astray; especially, through the lusts of the flesh. Pride comes in very handy as it can be very subtle. Anybody who says pride cannot affect them is already lost.

Jesus Christ said to His disciples when they asked Him to help them increase their faith that if they have faith as small as a mustard seed (Matthew 17:20), they would say to a mountain to be removed into the sea and it would obey them. This tells us that faith is not a matter of what we think or wish in the human sense.

Faith it is a matter of believing upon the Name of Jesus that whatever we ask the Father in the Name of Jesus Christ is as sure and good as already delivered.

Faith is being sure of what you hope for and certain of what you have not seen (Hebrews 11:1); not a matter of believing what you see or already have. Hebrews 11 deals so excellently with this as well as other aspects of the Holy Scriptures of course. It is well worth applying yourself to the study of any references in this book. Whatever you do, remember that without faith, no man can please God.

The Holy Spirit

The Holy Spirit is the Enabler. He Comes to fill the believer. He Enables the impossible to be achievable, even the living of a life pleasing unto God. In serious anguish, Samuel Taylor Coleridge (1772 – 1834) of Ottey St Mary Parish Church declared that Christianity is not a theory, or a speculation, but a life; not a philosophy of life, but a life and living process. How apt. For him, deep thinking is attainable only by a man of deep feeling. He surely struggled with his faith; but declared in his later years that with his heart, he never did abandon the Name of Jesus Christ.

God is a Spirit (John 4:24) and all who worship Him must worship Him in Spirit and in Truth. Although we many not see Him, being a Spirit, God knows all things and Can Do all things. God is to be Hallowed, Revered, Honoured. Many fail to remember that God is a Spirit.

Who is man to question God? Why do the nations rage against Him? God does not yield to human manipulations and "spoilt" behaviour and attitudes. We love to play clever and be politically correct with one another and try this on with God. However, we often forget that even before we came up with the ideas in our heads, God Knew. How else can what is created make judgements about and criticise the One who created the created? God knows all regardless.

Many people, including very well known preachers of the Word of God speak and act as if God's Holy Spirit never existed before the Acts 2 experience on the day of Pentecost. I know some will like to twist even my words now. However, do not get me wrong. I am saying that God is Holy. God is Righteous. As much as God is all these, God is a Spirit. When you put these two attributes of God together, for this particular purpose, you must come to understand that God cannot be anything but Holy.

When King David spoke of God in the Psalms, he spoke of God's Righteousness, Holiness etc. Surely, this is also reflected in the New Testament experience and not exclusive of the Old Testament. I shall revisit this matter shortly.

Please note however that the Pentecostal Advent of the Holy Spirit is a unique experience as Promised by the Risen Christ Jesus. According to the Apostle Paul in 1 Corinthians 2:12, we have not received the spirit of the world but the Spirit who is from God, that we may understand what God has freely given us. This great Gift from God is available to all who choose to become born again (John 3:5), that they may be edified and Led to live a holy life.

However, far less people were known to have been so enabled as in a public way by God in the past. Mostly, these were called servants of God – prophets, levites, specially gifted and talented people, say for building the Ark of the Covenant and the House of the Lord; or for waging war against the enemies of God.

The Spirit of God, from the beginning, is what has enabled great wonders. The Holy Spirit of God is the Enabler, manifested in diverse ways across the face of the earth over time periods. He is a Spirit Person and the speaking in tongues is what we did not read of in the Old Testament. God performed great wonders through His servants, some of which we have not witnessed since, like the parting of the Red Sea via Moses and of the Jordan via Joshua.

For the purposes of the Flaming Sword, God is Revealing Himself as a wholesome God, as expressed in Matthew 13:52, by Jesus Christ. Jesus said that every teacher of the law who has been Instructed about the Kingdom of Heaven is like the owner of a house who brings out of his storeroom new treasures as well as old.

God is Holy Spirit

The letter kills, but it is the Spirit that gives life (2 Corinthians 3:6). Of the writing of many books, there will never be an end. Too much study wearies the bones (Ecclesiastes 12:12). What is written is dead (both to the writer and the reader) unless the spirit of the letter comes alive (and the spirit of the writer's Inspiration).

We have God's Word backed up with His Authority that all Scripture is God Breathed and useful for admonition, instruction and teaching with regard to the way of righteousness and holiness of God (i.e. God's Way – 2 Timothy 3:16).

The letter may say even in your man-written dictionary that spirit and ghost mean the same thing (to man). However, from the deep roots of the meanings of these two words, they are clearly different in meaning.

Parakletos (Greek from which Holy Spirit was originally translated) does not and never will and never did translate into ghost at all. A ghost is not and cannot be holy. Those who worship ghosts will tell you freely that this cannot be possible. I have been researching this issue for several years and to date, God's Word is confirmed to and in me that Holy Spirit is not a ghost even as God is a Spirit and not a ghost. Nowhere in the Old Testament is God's Spirit referred to as a ghost.

The words spirit and ghost may be used in the worldly English language. However Spiritual Language must differ because a ghost is a dismembered spirit emanating from a dead body. When anyone who died is seen again, mostly people agree that when seen, it is that person's ghost that was seen. People talk of the spirit of their loved ones being with them at events. However, the

Bible says that it is appointed, once, to die; and after that, judgment (Hebrews 9:27).

God's Holy Spirit is a Spirit alright, but a Good, Living Spirit surely. On the other hand, a ghost is a type of spirit alright, but a dead one. Surely, nothing dead can be holy; for, when Jesus Christ was Crucified and He died, He was Raised from the dead and now, Jesus Christ Lives forever, for death could never hold Him captive.

Therefore, it is very well mistaken and erroneous to continue to refer to the Holy Spirit as holy ghost. No ghost can be holy.

It is totally inappropriate to ascribe what is unholy to a God who is Absolutely HOLY. Even our so called leaders and learned folk arrogantly hold onto what is clearly error, despite the efforts of the wise to make appropriate corrections.

The English Language recognises this fact even today, hence the final agreement to implement the written recommendation of the translators of the King James Version of the Holy Scriptures to make relevant amendments which include this matter of using the appropriate words to convey the right meaning of the Holy Spirit in the New King James Version. I am not making any recommendations of one version over another here, but stressing the importance and need for change.

The Spirit of God operates right through the Old Testament. Is the Spirit of God different from the Holy Spirit? Clearly not. The Spirit of God is the Holy Spirit. The One who was with Elijah and took him up such that he did not die. The same Spirit took Enoch and was upon God's servants all through the Holy Scriptures. God is not a ghost and must be revered.

We apply words in various modes of communication. The word ghost is not a good word as per the things of God (Holy God).

When people say they saw a ghost, the terror is very evident in their account of their experience.

There are two types of spirits (good and bad). There is no in-between. God hates anyone who is cold and lukewarm. In the worship of God through Jesus Christ, God wants for us to be hot. Likewise, we are encouraged to be holy and perfect not half holy and half perfect all through the Holy Scriptures. God being Holy must be Good. Therefore God's Spirit is very clearly HOLY SPIRIT (GOOD). Amen.

Nowhere in the Holy Scriptures is God referred to as a ghost except in false translations re: "holy ghost" which is essentially a veritable contradiction. A ghost can never be holy, being of its very nature/essence, something that emanates only from a dead body. Anything dead cannot be holy. Our God is a God of the living and not the dead; even as only the living can praise the Lord (Matthew 22:31-32). Jesus Christ Himself proclaimed accordingly.

All through the Holy Scriptures, God has been referred to as a Spirit, never a ghost. A ghost is unreal, cannot live and will never live, let alone forever; and is with no life potential at all. Holy Spirit in Jesus Christ is forever and ever. Amen. Jesus Christ who is authoritatively the Word of God, is essentially God. He declared that a ghost/spirit does not have flesh and bones as He had when He walked on the water and demonstrated this when Thomas queried (Luke 24:39; Matthew 14:25-26). This was after He Rose from the dead and before ascending unto Heaven.

Jesus Christ is alive forevermore. Amen. Therefore, God the Father, Son and Holy Spirit as revealed in the Holy Scriptures is HOLY SPIRIT. This is reflected right through the Old and New Testament (Holy Scriptures). This is an unchangeable fact. Let anyone who is a true follower of Jesus Christ acknowledge this.

God the Father Created the whole universe and mankind and all things in the world and in the heavens and all. God the Son is authoritatively the Wisdom of God and was present when this happened and was in God Himself. God the Son is authoritatively God, who came in the flesh (to our world, to humanity) that we may have salvation in being reconciled back to God. This fact of faith is a veritable belief; and attests to our faith in Jesus Christ, Son of God. It is written that in the beginning was the Word and the Word was with God and the Word was God and the Word became flesh (John 1:1-15).

The Holy Bible says very clearly that whomsoever believes in the Son has the Father; and whomsoever does not, has not the Father. Such is the antichrist (1 John 2:22-24). Hence, no one who does not believe in the Father and the Son being One can have the Holy Spirit. Holy Spirit is given unto those with the revelation of Jesus Christ as God, who continue in the fear of God, to live a holy life and in obeisance to the Direction of the Holy Spirit's Guidance.

Jesus Christ died publicly (crucified), was buried; and rose again on the third day. He showed Himself to over five hundred of His disciples and ascended into Heaven in the presence of several of them (alive). He is alive forevermore and promised that He would return. His Holy Angels (two of them) assured the disciples accordingly at the site/time of His Ascension. Jesus Christ also promised to send His Holy Spirit.

On the day called Pentecost (Acts 2), His Holy Spirit Came down as tongues of fire upon the one hundred and twenty of His Disciples who met in obedience to His Instruction at an agreed upper room. They obeyed. They expected faithfully. God delivered.

The event of this Pentecost day Outpouring of the Holy Spirit as prophesied and promised by Jesus Christ is authoritatively Truthful Evidence of the fulfilment of Jesus Christ's being God, having attained unto Victory over death completely and unto the Seating at the Right Hand of God in Heaven, from where the Holy Spirit could be Sent to His Disciples. Halleluyah! Amen.

Jesus Christ essentially prophesied that the world would not see Him after a while but that the disciples would (John 14), after His return to the Father. Specifically, He said that it is for their (and our) benefit that He had to go to the Father, so as to Send the promised Holy Spirit to His disciples and us of course who believe their testimony.

When Jesus prayed, He prayed for Himself, His own disciples and those who would believe them – very specific (John 17). Jesus Christ did not pray for the world. He prayed as God for God's followers. Only the Father can Send the Holy Spirit. Only the Father has that Authority.

Hence, to consolidate Jesus Christ's Fatherhood, He made clear that He had to return to the Godhead position to be Able to Send the Holy Spirit in His Name. He said that whatever the believer asks the Father in His (Jesus') Name will be done unto any who dare to believe and such shall do exploits.

Therefore, Jesus Christ Ascended to His Godhead (Father mode) – for no man can sit at the Right Hand of God and remain alive. God lives in unapproachable Light (1 Timothy 6:16). The testaments of scientists to the dangers of even getting close to the various heavens above the earth prove this point beyond any doubts. We can feel the heat of the sun even on earth here. Blessed be the Great God forevermore. Amen.

Jesus Christ clearly presented the Holy Spirit's coming (soon they would see Him He had said) as Himself not leaving the disciples as orphans, but will surely come to them. Therefore they testified that Jesus Christ and the Power of His Resurrection (Holy Spirit) are One and the same. Only God Can Send and Manifest as the Holy Spirit in the life of any man. Whatever the true believer asks the

Father in the Name of Jesus Christ the Son shall be done through the Power of the Holy Spirit for they are One.

God is One with Jesus Christ. As God is Holy, God is the Holy Spirit; Jesus Christ, Son of God is Holy Spirit. As Jesus Christ is in the Godhead, He is Spirit and He is Holy. Jesus Christ is Perfect (as on earth) in Heaven. Only God is Perfect and only God can lead any man into all Truth and all Righteousness and Holiness (work of the Holy Spirit).

Beyond any doubts whatsoever, all who are in Christ Jesus, Blessed with His Holy Spirit, must know and be assured fully that God the Father, Son and Holy Spirit are One. Therefore, God is Holy Spirit and by His very nature cannot be otherwise. Ascribe Greatness and Holiness to our God the King. It is a most dishonourable thing to ascribe the word ghost to our Most Holy and Righteous God. God is a Spirit; and again I say that all who worship Him must do so in Spirit and in Truth (John 4:24), through Jesus Christ our Lord. Amen.

This is why without holiness no one will see the Lord (Hebrews 12:14); even as without faith no one can please God (Hebrews 11:6). Our God is an awesome God. Mankind are filled with dread when there is none to dread (Psalm 53:5); yet the One who is Himself Dreadful is dishonoured. Dread must belong to God as it is part of His Being to be Dreaded. Dread is awesome fear. God alone is able to destroy all regardless. He alone is to be feared. Fear God folks and obey His Word.

Of the Church...

Before anyone can come to be a part of the Body of Christ Jesus, (referred to as the Church), the person must be fully assured of all the above-discussed and be willing to fully submit to God's Will through the Guidance of the Holy Spirit. The true believer must be transformed. The evidence is not just spiritual (internal), but physical (external). The proof of this is in the fact that such people were observed, known and called followers of Christ, later referred to as Christians (first at Antioch – Acts 11:25-26).

The future of the believer is no longer in his hands; but rather as determined by the Holy Spirit. Jesus made this very clear in saying that as the wind blows and no one knows where it came from nor its destination, so shall it be with those that are born of the (Holy) Spirit (John 3:7-9). The Bible further clarifies that as many as are led by the Spirit of God, these are the sons of the Living God (Romans 8:13-15). Not all are sons of the Living God; but those who are led by His Holy Spirit. They stand out, reflecting this leading in a unique way.

The dead cannot praise the Living God. God is a God of the living (Matthew 22:32; Mark 12:27). Although God Can do as He purposes with all (regardless of death), God is essentially a God of the living and not of the dead, as only the living can praise Him. God is not a God of the dead. God is a God of the living and God is a Living God as surely as our Lord Jesus Christ lives forever. Jesus Christ is the Lord God Almighty. We want to live and not die. When in the Lord, whether alive or dead, Jesus Christ is your Lord; for to Him, even though you die, yet you shall live (Luke 20:38).

Any who die in Christ Jesus; though dead, shall yet live again in Jesus Christ. For the Lord Jesus Christ is coming back again

(Revelations 22:7) and the dead in Christ shall surely rise first (1 Thessalonians 4:16). It is very important to note that God is a God of the living as stated in the Holy Scriptures. We struggle hard not to die – when Jesus said that whoever wants to keep his life will die but whoever will give his life for Jesus' sake will attain unto Eternal Life. Our priorities are warped; we need Jesus.

Hence, the true follower of Jesus Christ must be a living stone (1 Peter 2:5). The Holy Temple of God is a Living Temple. This is why Jesus Christ Himself is the Head and Chief Cornerstone (Ephesians 2:20). So the world today tends to freely abuse the word Church as much as we abuse the word Love and indeed as much as we abuse the Living God in Jesus Christ Himself.

For our sakes, even us who claim to believe, because we do our own will as against seeking after the Holy Spirit for God's Will so as to do His Will, we lack the fear of God to do His Will, hence, the world profanes our God and His Glorious Name, even Jesus Christ. To be a living stone demands great and faithful commitment, devotion and dedication to obey God not just when we want, but always.

You may mouth being born again, but when we come to Jesus, we must prove our repentance (Acts 26:20) in thoughts, words and deeds commensurate with the Light which has come into our lives. Jesus said by their deeds you shall know them.

This is about a clear change in our lives, following after the likeness of Jesus Christ through the renewal of our minds. All things must become new. We cannot continue to live as we did and claim to be born again. By continuing in sin and not allowing God to deal with the old self, we profane the Lord's Name.

As in the parable of the sower (Mark 4; Matthew 13), the new believer must die to sin. The old self must die (Romans 6:6). Only then can the true believer bear good fruits, fruits that last. Jesus Christ wants for us to bear fruits that last (John 15:16). The true believer must die;

be buried, raised and ascend (be seated with Christ in Heavenly places) in Truth. There is no short cut to becoming a disciple of Jesus Christ. Jesus commanded us who believe to go and make disciples of all men in every nation (Matthew 28:19).

The Lord Jesus Christ has been telling me for many years that what we call church today is not His Church. He said He is Building His Church and the gates of hell shall not ever prevail against His Church (Matthew 16:18).

I urge my reader who claims to be part of the Church of Jesus Christ to test and re-test yourself and your faith. Check to see that you are in the Faith and that you are a part of the Church. The enemy has sown tares amongst the wheat. Be wise. Do not give in to false teaching.

As touched on earlier on in dealing with the issue of who believes and has faith (Of Faith…), it is very essential to then know what the church is or not, as there is now too much confusion around the issue of religion, church and the world (secular or not).

Although tares may be sown amongst the wheat, the Body of Jesus Christ is made up of true believers and nothing else. Tares will never stand the test of time. Hence, not part of the Church. Satan will never be part of the Church. Satan may and has sown seeds amongst those who (claim to) believe. Hence, what we see as and call church is not seen as Church by God at all.

Jesus Christ made clear in His Word that He is coming back for a Church without blemish. When anyone has passed from worldliness into willingly submitting to the Will of God to be born again and Led by the Holy Spirit, such a person's desires will change and he will only want to please God (Romans 8:8; Galatians 1:10; 1 Thessalonians 4) and desire strongly to do so more and more daily.

Earnestly pray for Holy Spirit's Help so as not to sin or continue to gratify the sinful nature (Romans 8:5-9). This new person will no longer wish to yield to the evil youthful desires that fulfil only the fleshly, sinful nature. Thus the true believer emerges even as the old man is shed. It is not for the believer to crave the world (James 4:4) so much as to be like the world in practically all ways and sing and shout daily about how born again we are.

These who believe form the Body of Christ. Believers are the bride of Christ Jesus; not just anyone claiming to believe, rather, God approved. As the Holy Bible says that it is not those who men commend and or approve that stand justified before God, rather, those whom God commends (2 Corinthians 10:17-18).

Many who claim a part of the Church of Jesus Christ have no part at all in Him for He Knows them not. Faith in Jesus Christ is manifested physically. It is the beauty of Jesus Christ and not of our adulterous crafting of idolatry that identifies the believer. We humans love to acclaim one another, especially our friends or those of the same ilk as us.

A true believer is not moved by or in search after man's acclaim; but in all things and ways seeks to please God through diligent seeking out for (Hebrews 11:6) and obedience to the Word of God respectively, in Jesus Christ. Amen.

Of Sanctification....

I have touched on the body being the temple of the Living God. The Bible tells us that God requires that we present our bodies unto Him, holy and acceptable in His sight – this is our spiritual act of sacrifice (Romans 12:1). We cannot thus do with our bodies or parts of them what we like and choose. We cannot unite with prostitutes or unholiness. We are urged to come out from the world and not be unequally yoked with the world (2 Corinthians 6:14).

A reflective look at so-called Christians today, who claim to be born again, shows that, they are more worldly than the world at large in disposition. They try even harder than the world to be like the world. They look like the world, think like the world and act as the world in almost every facet of life – men and women alike, but in particular our women. We lead our children by example, likewise.

Our men desire the world and lust after the world. The women love that and try hard to outdo each other in the way of the world, hiding behind various masks like masquerades and yet claiming to be of God. We attend for church and are part of practically all activities etc. but few want to partake of the fellowship with the suffering of Jesus Christ in terms of self-discipline (Romans 8:17; Philippians 3:10; 1 Peter 4:13).

So-called leaders and teachers (male and female) lead multitudes astray and yet although the Holy Scriptures warn against this trend and eventual falling away and following after lying spirits/demons taught by depraved teachers whose judgement has been set, multitudes follow after them (Mark 13:22; Matthew 7:15; 2 Peter 2).

The Bible especially says of women that they shall be sanctified (and or saved) through child bearing if they continue in faith, love and holiness with propriety (1 Timothy 2:15). Today we have all sorts of women who claim to believe, not even wanting to have children at all; and some choosing not the natural way of childbirth (therefore avoiding child bearing) but going through with pregnancy and the child removed from their womb by doctors. They thereby miss out on the promise through their own choices.

Likewise, the fear of God and Godly discipline through which a person is taught the Way of God in Jesus Christ, is absent in many men and women, because all are largely after worldly success, which has now become the standard (yardstick) of what is perceived to be successful Christianity. We now call the arrogant blessed (Malachi 3:15). This is not Biblical and is contrary to God's Word which clearly says to seek first the Kingdom of God and His righteousness. Then all things shall be added unto the believer. Of course, needs, not necessarily wants (Matthew 6:33).

Of the body of the believer, the Bible says that in this body (temple) reside all sorts of articles (of wood and of clay; gold and silver). Those of the former are said to be for ignoble purposes whilst the latter are for noble purposes. As a person wilfully and continuously rids himself of the former and therefore enables the latter to increase , such persons become instruments of value, worthy of Godly use for every good work in the Name and Spirit of Jesus Christ (2 Timothy 2:19-21).

Not all are automatically instruments of righteousness, useful to the Master (Jesus Christ). However, God Can use anyone for the fulfilment of His Will. Anyone submitted to the Will of Jesus Christ must go through the renewing of their minds (Romans 12:2) and this will manifest in the new man in thoughts words and deeds.

Today, what we see largely is the opposite. This is very serious and those who want to follow Jesus and all those who are following Jesus must be very careful to stand firm and continue in the Way (1 Corinthians 10:12, 15:58; Mark 13:13; Philippians 1:27). The study of the Word of God (2 Timothy 2:13-15) is a most essential endeavour for the believer. This allows the roots of God's disciplined, faithful love, to be deeply entrenched in the believer.

Studying includes continuous meditation and reflection as David espouses excellently in the Psalms. When a person is determined to fully commit to the Word of God in thoughts, words and deeds, the Holy God through Jesus Christ Will take notice. Holy Scriptures say that the Angels of God (ministering spirits of God) encamp around those who fear God and tremble at His every Word (Psalm 34:7; Isaiah 66:2). This tells of those fully committed to seeking and following after God's Way.

Our Lord Jesus Christ learnt obedience from the things He suffered. We must go through the fire of purification (Daniel 11:25; Daniel 12:10). God did not spare Jesus Christ the agony of the Cross. How could we think that we could take only the sweet of the world and add onto that the sweet of the Great God and expect to be automatically translated into Heaven? We are quite willing and wanting to go to Heaven but none of us want to die. God is a Good God, true; but God will not compromise His Holy Word for sinful man.

Wake up O mankind and acknowledge your Creator. The time is coming (and soon) when all opportunities shall cease and all doors shut and all that will be left will be Judgment that cannot be changed. Jesus said as it was in the days of Noah, so shall it be when He Returns (Matthew 24:37). Are you ready for the coming of Jesus Christ?

Jesus Christ...
The Way, Truth and Life

The above is made very clear in the Holy Scriptures (John 14:6). Yet, although revealed especially in the New Testament, the roots are essentially of Old and revealed right through the Old Testament. Many find this very hard to take in. Even today's so called Christians and the true believer must be careful to seek after God's Heart to follow His Will faithfully. I am stating authoritatively that Jesus Christ is the Ancient of Days (Daniel 7:9-23), with His Roots of Old, although Revealed in the New Testament.

The Law and Prophets prove this repeatedly as well as the Gospels do right through with links drawing both together right through to the Book of Revelation in the Bible.

Prophet Jeremiah in Chapter 6:16-18 of the Holy Bible confirms this in directing people to follow the Ancient Paths; you will probably agree with me that only the Ancient Paths lead to the Ancient of Days. Jesus Christ Himself in Matthew 13:52 spoke clearly regarding the value of the Old and New Testaments. Jesus made clear too that He did not come to abolish the Law, but to fulfil the Law (Matthew 5:17).

The Ten Commandments (Deuteronomy 5) for example may be difficult for the ordinary man to practically live out daily, but the Holy Spirit was Sent to Enable Holy Living. No one can live a holy life unless God Helps through the intervention of the Holy Spirit (Acts 9:31).

Yet, the now infamous exposition of the Ten Commandments in what is the Mosaic Laws, were a veritable guide for the children of

God, the Jews. To ignore these guides for living life in God through Jesus Christ is perilous error.

Jesus Christ did not ever discount them, only further summarised them. The Commandments are a summary of God's laws exposed in the Mosaic Laws. Jesus said that to love the Lord our God (with all our hearts etc.) and love our neighbours as ourselves is all that is needful (Matthew 22:36-40).

However, reflecting on these issues further, Jesus Christ explained that basically, it is our lack of love that makes us sin. If we love one another, having love first for our own selves, we would not want (or give in) to sin against one another. Hence, love covers a multitude of sins (James 5:20; 1 Peter 4:8).

That Jesus Christ is the Way is made abundantly clear in our being urged (as a must) to be born again. That He is the Truth likewise, in the Sending of the Holy Spirit to Lead us into all Truth and Righteousness. Finally, that Jesus Christ is the Life is made manifest in that whomsoever eats of His Flesh and drinks of His Blood, believing in the Son of Man (God), is one who has the life (John 6:53). Even though such die, yet will he live.

Of the Way....

Jesus Christ declared with Power that He is the Way. Now we must understand that this profound statement (I am the Way, the Truth and the Life) was never made before, or after, by any human (to date), male or female. Indeed, many humans feel that their path is okay for them. There are many paths that humans follow after today; whatever journey a person does undertake in life is the way they chose.

The Holy Scriptures say that there is a way that seems right to a man, in the end it leads to death (Proverbs 16:25). The popular culture in any part of the world is filled with throngs of people that revel in it. These cultures come with associated dos and don'ts. To fit in, one must be willing to abide with and follow after the dos and don'ts as well as the associated requirements (and or pros and cons). Often you have to (because you are expected to) do things that you would not dream of doing normally.

There goes a saying that everybody does it so it doesn't matter (until the fruits manifest of course). As it happens, whether we like it or not, we walk and tread certain particular paths in life that will serve as our seed-sowing. Seeds sown will in turn yield a sure harvest in due season (good or bad). Whatever we sow we shall eventually reap (Galatians 6:7).

No one sows or plants onions and reaps tomatoes; likewise, no one plants vegetables and reaps roses. God cannot be mocked at all. Whatever seeds we sow, from that we shall reap (not another). Access is what the Way is about. Jesus Christ is the only access to the Father. Even in hearing (Romans 10:13-15), the Word of God (manifested in the Holy Bible) urges that we take care how we hear

(Mark 4:23-25); for the simple reason that seeds are sown based upon what is registered on the mind. These also bear fruits.

If only humans would take the time to reflect and meditate on the Word of God. A statement like the second to the last one in the previous paragraph becomes very life threatening indeed. How do we hear today, in this world of advertising, when the power of suggestion is very much used in witchcraft to divert our focus from anything Godly onto whatever the witches, satanists, sorcerers etc. want us to focus on?

Not all that glitters is indeed gold. There is deception in the air. I hope my reader would understand me when I urge that you watch and pray for the times are foul. Hence, when we become born again and baptised into Jesus Christ, we must go through a renewing of the mind. This can only be done successfully in full submission to the Holy Spirit who is Sent to Lead us into all Truth and all Righteousness.

Of Truth...

Human beings arrogantly declare that truth is relative to the beholder. This debate goes on endlessly amongst mankind. Statements like your truth is not my truth and vice-versa are not at all uncommon. This is to say that everyone has their own truth.

What I find interesting is that the legal profession have very global (international) standards across the range of applicable professional lines. Perhaps we may call these the legal truths, but not the Truth. We may have excellent publications and call such the witches' bible, legal bible, etc.; these differ totally from the Holy Bible.

Truth is Truth. Darkness has no power over Truth. Truth always prevails. Truth is a function of time; in time, Truth prevails. As Light prevails over darkness (no competition), Truth prevails over all falsehood. Indeed, Truth is Light. All followers of Jesus Christ (the Way) eventually come into the knowledge of the Truth; and all who have the Way and the Truth enter into Life.

The opposite of truth is lie. Satan is the father of all lies and all liars too. Liars always oppose truth as they obey their father. Lying leads to a lot of evil. Ultimately, it is most beneficial that Truth prevails in our lives. Invite Truth into your life and love Him. Then you shall know the Truth and the Truth shall set you free (John 8:31-33).

Of Life...

Life is Eternal. Life is alive and shall never die. Life is a dynamic force. The seed of life is live and even though it dies, this is only a transformation. As in all seeds, before it can live, first it has to die. Yet, to die in this way is not our human understanding of dying.

Plant any seed and you soon discover that although a process of death is effected for that seed, it is actually in a process of profound transformation into life and even so, more abundantly. The seeds sown eventually yield a harvest, bearing much fruit, producing more seeds which go through the same process.

Quantum physics cannot ever explain why the sum total of equal forces far greatly exceeds their sum total in terms of energy generated when applied together in any particular direction, with regard to the total value of power/force added up and applied.

Tests prove that the force/power generated by the total amount of energy added together and applied far greatly exceeds the expectations of the observer, researcher and or scientist in terms of mathematical calculations and predictions. The force generated far exceeds their wildest imaginations.

The impact of this experiment with regard to the outcome is very exciting. I see Life in this sense where Jesus Christ is Life. Whatever we have or do not have, when we apply faith, our results, outcomes and or natural expectations are absolutely and overwhelmingly exceeded. The Bible says that in Jesus Christ, we have life, even more abundantly (John 10:10).

Whatever is of life stands out in everyway. So many times I have observed mankind and studied their faces as they go about daily matters without fail. At such times I fear God so much. I see death in the eyes and faces of most. I have talked to many too and my perception very similar. It makes me fear God more. Are you alive today? Do you know that many know that they are dead really, just living for emptiness?

Many will eventually break down and even the hardest would weep when faced with the love of Jesus. Some run; for they never knew love for real before. Before casting judgements, perhaps all should reflect on themselves. Do we have life? What are we spreading daily? Life or death? From the above, it is safe to conclude that life cannot die. What dies is not eternal and cannot be. Life is an eternal continuum. Death is only a catalyst along this continuum. This is why scientists can never fathom the concept of God; for God is Supremely Dynamic in every sense of the word.

Of God and Love...

I will like to deal with love at this stage because God is Love (1 John 4:8). God is revealed in the Holy Scriptures as all Knowing (Omniscient), all Powerful (Omnipotent – Revelation 19:6), all Kind (Omni-benevolent) and all Present (Omnipresent). This reminds one instinctively of our discussion around Life, which as espoused above, generates tremendous power.

God, we must agree must be greatly powerful beyond all imagination. God is inherently Perfect in Love, Power, Righteousness and in all ways (Matthew 5:48).

The Holy Bible reveals God as Love. Love is flawless. Love is pure and without blemish. These attributes very surely resonate with Truth in the transparency of purity. When taken simply as is evident and manifested in the Holy Scriptures, Love is very easily understandable. Where we fail is in application.

Love is very clearly stronger than death as love lives on long after death and love is light and not darkness. Love cannot be darkened. Love always brings light and never darkness in the bearer, both in countenance and in response.

In saying that God is Love, one is saying that Love is powerful beyond all. Love covers a multitude of sins as made clear in the Holy Bible. Love overcomes all (1 Corinthians 13) and there is nothing impossible for Love as God is Love and there is nothing impossible for God.

God's Love is the Power of God. As God is Love, God's Power will never cease to flow wherever love flows. Hence, we are greatly urged and admonished in Scriptures to love one another (John 13:33-35; John 15:12-18), starting with a fervent love for God.

Humans find it hard to love a God they cannot see. Yet, all who have dared to understand, to learn, to comprehend God and know Him end up falling completely in love with God. The more anyone will draw near to God, the more they will draw near to love. The more love is made known to anyone, the more love reveals each person's heart. Love is a life source and resource that opens up all dark alleys in the person. As darkness is revealed by love, love increases in effecting change in the person.

No matter how much a person hates or dislikes even him/herself, love changes their disposition completely and they begin to have respect and love for how God the Almighty Creator has made them. Otherwise, no one can love one another as one's self; especially when the individual does not love their own self.

God is Omnipotent, Omniscient, Omnibenevolent and Omnipresent; i.e. All Powerful, All Knowing, All Kind and All Present (present everywhere at the same time). A lot can be written about love, for God is Love par excellence.

Loving God the Creator...

Now, many may not wish to call God God. I am focusing this bit on those willing to (at least) try for the purpose of exploring the facts of creation available in all of history and science etc. These point to the fact that a Force brought about life on earth and or in the whole universe. We encounter God in creation every way, every day. God's dynamism, His invisible qualities have been clearly made know from time immemorial so that we make no excuses for not honouring Him to whom all honour is due (Romans 1:18-20).

There is too much to see and share in terms of examples to give in support of the Truth that I hold alongside many others that there is indeed a God, who created all things excellently and in absolute perfection. We may argue that there are imperfections in creation; e.g. freaks of nature etc. However, to deny the awesome excellence of creation as we see it unfold each passing day, is to deny Truth and deny the existence of God.

The Bible rightly shows us that God has indeed given us more than enough in creation to prove His Reality; not just in, but, as life. Clearly not all will or can believe. I cannot but be thankful that it has been acknowledged, even amongst those who do not believe in God, that the magnitude of numbers of those in the world who have faith in God in one way or other is too convincingly overwhelming to discard the notion of God as irrelevant in this world.

Drawing near to God...

Is it not interesting that when we teach children or seek to do so, we consciously keep our efforts simple and as straightforward as possible? This enables the children to understand quickly and begin to obey what we instruct them not to do or to do and to put their learning to practice. Keeping their learning simple and straightforward makes their learning easier and better to retain in their memory.

It is likewise interesting that children are very easy to teach only for the humble, patient and willing. Love plays a key part in teaching children for they respond naturally to loving and caring in the learning process. If not loved and cared for very sensitively, children will likely be damaged in some way or other and end up tuning off the learning process. They will just clam up, shut; until the power of love brings healing again to them, thereby restoring their confidence in the learning process.

For now, we are on the issue of drawing near to God (Hebrews 10:21-23). We have a veritable manual in the Holy Bible. God urges us to come as little children (Matthew 18:2-4) in our approach to His Word. Firstly, to love Him with all we have (clearly stated in the very first of the Ten Commandments in Deuteronomy 5:7).

It is no use drawing near to God unless one is interested genuinely to know the Truth about Him. That is to say one must be sincere in spirit.

As God is a Spirit, all who worship Him must do so in spirit and in truth (John 4:23). But only those who dare to draw near (close) to Him, to learn to know Him, will be able to enjoy this privilege.

If you are willing, daring and sincere (Matthew 11:12), then seek after Him for yourself, determined to succeed step by step in unravelling the mystery and excitement of knowing Him. You never know what you will meet along the way; but be assured that drawing near to God is a worthy challenge that will set you on fire for love and set you free in learning to know God through Jesus Christ.

You will thus come to know and understand the Truth, once for all. The Bible makes clear that when you draw near to God, He Will Draw near to you. What a revelation this is for any truth seeker.

This is not to say that it is easy to do so. But what have you to lose in drawing near to God? You get some more light to reveal more darkness that you must let go of. So what? Shame is nothing when God is setting you free. Be bold and let God do it. God alone loves you enough to keep at you when all else fails. He said He will not leave nor forsake you (Deuteronomy 31:6; Joshua 1:5). God will not give up on you if you covenant with Him and trust in Him absolutely. Come to Jesus Christ and know life. Through Jesus Christ you will gain wisdom for life.

Of Truth and Freedom...

Oh what a great joy is mine that I have the privilege to come to the gradual and painful knowledge of Jesus Christ. Only through this arduous journey have I learnt the virtues of patience and love with perseverance in the face of diverse life adversities and persecution from God-haters and so-called God-lovers alike. Truth is in Jesus Christ and is Him.

This Truth is different and I strongly urge anyone to search far and wide and leave nothing undone, no stones unturned, to get the knowledge of the Truth. There is a great joy awaiting anyone who makes this commitment in the utmost sincerity of heart – to know Truth. Jesus Christ said in His Word that we should come to Him in love and purity as little children. We are strongly encouraged to come to Jesus in a sincere transparency of intent.

If we are willing and wilfully obey His Word, Commandments and instructions, we prove thereby that we love Him and we shall know the Truth and the Truth shall set us free (John 8:31-33). We must remember of course, that Jesus Christ is the Truth and only He can set us free. Most human beings are in very dire situations on a day to day basis; and in serious bondage of diverse complex dimensions.

We are bound in sin onto all sorts of fetishes, idols, addictions, afflictions, evil devices etc., all of which take a great toll on us. Yet, we remain as though we do not have a choice to opt for the Way (of Truth) to Life.

Yet, we do have this choice, which although given to us so we can wilfully and willingly choose God and not satan, good and never evil, we are always predisposed to choosing that which is satanic, worldly, ungodly and evil (bad) to our own detriment (Romans 7:7-25). Hence the entrapment of worldly, even youthful pleasures and desires. We are as such heavily yoked with the world of darkness, ruled by satan, prince of this world (John 12:30-32; Revelations 12:8-10).

Our love for the world only serves as a cover that thickens, the deeper we enter into the world and accept what it has to offer. Over time, we become calloused in our hearts. The heart then hardens over time and there is increasing need to cover up more and more in our daily lives. We lose any inhibitions against sinning. Guilt trips abound and we blame everyone else (including God) except ourselves.

I call this fake living; a masquerading of Revealed Truth in everyday living. We hide in thoughts words and deeds. We hide in garments and false praises from so called friends and enemies alike.

Of Masks... with regard to Truth and Freedom

We wear all sorts of masks and are full of false pretences in our outward dispositions, revelling in our "sweet" sinfulness. We forget that our body is the temple of the Living God. We dress immorally and are never satisfied with how God made us; hence, the insatiable drive to please the human nature in "helping" God to "look better". We need to change, since we are fearfully and wonderfully made (Psalm 139:13-15), created in the image of God (Genesis 1:26-28).

This reminds me of the African masquerades. Some are so horrible looking, but nevertheless fantastic works of art. There is so much "magic" involved that not just anyone can wear them; certainly, hardly any women as far as I know up till the time of writing this message.

They are images of the most pathetic nature sometimes; and yet, with great pomp, pageantry and high spirits, people wear them nevertheless. Likewise the African saying that humans sometimes hide behind one finger – a type of self-deception; even as an ostrich buries her head in the sand, leaving the body out, yet feeling as though hidden from danger. Regardless, we love them. We live and die in our pledges to honour and continue in the worshipping of these idols and teach our children likewise.

In the traditional cultural sense, masquerades are supposed to excite and scare – for fun and sometimes punishment etc. A combination of emotions are attached to this very mythical idolatry; practiced amongst many peoples of the world, with such vigour, vitality and faithfulness that belies normal thinking.

Another example is the "carnival" celebrations worldwide, some of which are simply outrageous to say the least; nevertheless, beautiful to the human eye. The dedication to these phenomena is simply awe-inspiring; considering how little we actually celebrate God in Jesus Christ, who died for us.

Likewise, we help God to make us look better. Makeovers galore; jewelleries, wigs, unnatural hair-dos, make-up kits, face lifts, plastic surgeries, tummy tucks, face and or skin bleaching, tattooing, body piercing, joints, smoking, alcohol, drugs, fine oils and perfumes, fine clothing and power dressing etc. The list is simply endless.

There is nothing we would not do to our bodies for various purposes. Even our men dress their hair as the women; this, aside from dressing in women's clothing and vice-versa. We readily wear clothing of the opposite sex and engage in homosexual and or lesbian behaviours and support the same. We are now veritably and increasingly lascivious in our daily behaviour, with attending debauchery.

We have an unnatural desire for mirrors' commendations to let us know we are all right; yet, never satisfied. Even in terms of self-restraint in sexual activity, like dogs we are largely without restraint. Sexual immorality and attendant perversions are in our so-called churches, schools, work, meetings and homes.

We pretend that all is well whilst we promote yoga and various worldly teachings including the passing off as no big deal, issues around masturbation, homosexual and lesbian behaviours and other perverse, kinky sexual activities. We become obsessed with and increase in bodily exercises, which profit only a little bit according to the Holy Scriptures (1 Timothy 4:8), as against spiritual exercise. We do this even to gain sexy looks and bodies.

Our women stop breast feeding our children so their breasts will not become flabby. They want to have less or no children at all;

partly so their bodies will keep. They purchase surrogates to care for and nurture our children, against God's laid down procedures (1 Timothy 2:15; Titus 2:4-6) and nature itself, with attendant diversity of challenges.

Seduction galore at our prayer/church or other religious meetings, is a thing of great attraction to the world. Hence the lowering of the Standard of God, to allow for the world to freely dominate our so-called church meetings where our young men and women and even their mothers and fathers are increasingly as shrine prostitutes (2 Kings 23:7, Hosea 4:14) paraded for show. This has permeated what we call church choirs too.

We are now all for gospel music, presented as worldly as can be, as opposed to praises unto God. Even those charged with leading the flocks and with the custody of God's Word engage freely with and promote these worldly pursuits (covertly or otherwise). Now we want to take the church to the world and bring the world into the church, rather contrary to the Holy Scriptures.

Jesus Christ added to the numbers of believers in a totally different way (Acts 2:41; 5:14) and not in today's cosmetic and heavy marketing-gimmicks driven way. We have turned the freedom offered in Christ Jesus into an opportunity for a licence unto liberty to engage in sin (Galatians 5:13).

Entertainment has taken over from genuine praises and the competition is stiff for the right looks and clothing to fit in for the fashion and other shows. We have become the envy of the showbiz world in our drive to be successful. We are steeped in the world when the Bible says to come out from them (2 Corinthians 6:17).

We hide under various masks. We cover ourselves with prosperity teaching. Whatever happened to seeking first the Kingdom of God and His Righteousness? That appears to have taken a permanent back seat (Matthew 6:32-34). We claim the world in the Name of Jesus. We profane the Holy Name.

The "world" freely profane the Name of our God because of our behaviour (Ezekiel 13:19;). Yet, rather than repent in sackcloth and ashes (Malachi 3:14-16) we glorify sin freely, revel in our own glory, glorify each other and say God is a Gracious God. Yes He Is, but He is a Holy God and He hates sin. We hide under the Grace of God as though God condones sinfulness.

Where then do we draw the line? Should we continue to live in sin? The Bible says not. Should we say because it is difficult for us not to sin then make that as an excuse to encourage sin? I say not. Oh we hide in the Word of God too. We hear much of the don't judge me (Luke 6:37) phrase all over the place without any consideration for the Word of God. The Word of God is consistent.

This Word of God clearly tells us that the man of God shall be a judge of all things but be subject to no one's judgement (1 Corinthians 2:15). Alas, for the wrath of the Lord is upon the earth. The time is near and God's Word must be fulfilled. I know that I will be judged very harshly for this message, but that is just it; we are good at that, but most keep silent, when there is need to speak up on behalf of the Truth. The flesh opposes the Spirit of God (Galatians 5:16-18).

We have abandoned the True Faith and follow after lies and falsehoods, to our shame. We take the freedom offered by Jesus Christ as a new age type of freedom for which a dire price is paid always (even historically). We brazenly and shamelessly parade our sinfulness as though God loves sin. Before sanctification is made complete in any one, Jesus Christ must approve.

Sanctification is a continuous process. Rather, men and women commend each other (2 Corinthians 10:12-18) and various "cabals" exist. If you don't fit in you don't belong and will not be allowed in. You need a letter of commendation (2 Corinthians 3:1-3) to get "in".

There is discrimination in the so called church and any fair minded person who studies Scriptures will know that God is not in our many meetings and cannot ever be pleased with the way we comport ourselves in His Name. Has God changed? I say not. We often want nothing to do with the original traditional roots of the Christian Faith and reject any who try to correct us in this regard.

We make our own rules as we go along and anything we do not like takes a back seat as though God has no eyes to see our works. With great affront and audacious effrontery we condemn the likes of the Apostle Paul for the Inspiration God Gave him (Blessed him with) to give us directly from Jesus Christ Himself, attested to by God even through the Apostle Peter (2 Peter 3:15,16). We speak freely and rashly about things we do not understand (2 Peter 2:12).

Jesus Christ urged that we come to Him – all, like myself, who are weak and heavily laden (burdened) and He would give us Rest (Peace). Jesus Christ urged us to learn from Him for He is gentle and meek of spirit. He urged that we take His Yoke upon us for it is easy and His burden is light. He urged that we learn from Him. Jesus Christ offered us the wisdom/knowledge of His being of gentle disposition and meekness of heart (Matthew 11:28).

Such love, because it would take a disciplined continuous effort, has sincere attraction, only for a few. As a narrow road that leads to the Kingdom of God (even Heaven), few thus find it (Matthew 7:14). Yet, we carry on as if life will never end, rather than live as though each day were the last. We live a lie. We go on as though life is for the taking and love for the greedy. We forget that time is so short (I Corinthians 7:29).

On the earth, it is granted onto man, once to die and after that judgement (Hebrews 9:27). We shall all visit the Judgement Throne

one day and stand either to be Blessed and accepted into Eternal life forever or condemned to eternal damnation in hell, where the burning never stops (Mark 9:23; Revelation 20:10). It takes wisdom from God Himself through Jesus Christ to be truly free. To be free, you and I must drop the mask(s). They lead only onto death, not freedom. Only Jesus Christ can save and set free.

Beloved, we cannot keep the mask(s) on. It is not possible for us to worship God and mammon (Matthew 6:24). We cannot serve two masters. This is not possible; we must give up on one. If you are still serving satan in anyway or still have anything of his within you and or in your possession, satan will never leave you alone. Satan went after Jesus Christ. So, do not deceive yourself and say you can change anytime you like. Your mask has gradually become a part of you whether you know it or not; whether you like it or not.

The only way out is to drop the mask now. Give it up immediately. There is no point in prolonging the time, saying you do not have the will power. You do not need your own power anymore when you let Jesus Christ into your life. Do not wait till you understand fully. Testimonies abound regarding those whom Jesus Christ Touched. Like them all, you are weak but can rejoice because, in your weakness, the Power of our Lord Jesus Christ is made Perfect (2 Corinthians 12:9) for real.

Of Wisdom and the Fear of God...

Let me say this; a vast majority of the world's population cannot be all ignorant and deranged so as to behold God as Awesome and Great beyond measure in His Magnificence and Great Power. To be the Creator in a world that seeks after democracy, must be a great and worthy Enthronement, considering the futility of all the human fuss. So, let us agree that God is by far Superior to all in the role of Creator. No other one fits the Role and never will there be another.

Also, that Jesus Christ is the Son of God; and in Him is Revealed the absolute Being of God, both on earth and in Heaven, is a very Christian postulation. That Jesus Christ is Lord God Almighty, is simply "heavy" and awesome to behold. It is not a matter of whether it makes sense or not.

As the mystery of how a baby is formed in the womb is great; from the liquid state of male seed (semen) meeting with egg, to the development of the baby in the womb, in a breathing hearty state, with flesh and bones, so is the mystery of Jesus Christ. Yet, even as the baby being embedded in fluids within the mother's body is so real, it is so easy not to believe; except of course, that, when the time is ripe, the baby is born in a most spectacular way.

Once baby is born, from the state described, it is transformed into our mode of existence – the severing of the umbilical cord and the automatic inducing by either slapping of bottom or not, for the baby to cry out with the life force. No baby is known to speak in the womb or cry. Once born however, the baby begins to cry and breathe like us all. After a little while, the baby begins to babble, as if speaking in a language we do not know. This is simply awesome to behold. What sceptic can deny the reality of this process of birthing a baby into this world? Who can deny the reality of this new born? To deny Christ Jesus is to deny our very existence.

Therefore, although God gave eyes to us with ears, mouths with a tongue each, noses, hearts, minds, etc., to see, hear, breathe, smell, taste, believe, think, etc., in doubting Him, we deny our very own existence. All of these things and more that we spend our whole lives pondering would surely take a special appraisal to behold in truth. The reality of God is further evident in the very environment we live in. The climate, the changes, the oceans, seas, trees, animals, birds, insects, etc. – and all with their own modes of reproduction. From time immemorial, the reality of God has indeed been made known to humankind (Romans 1:20).

This is why it is so essential for mankind to do all possible to get knowledge and understanding; to spend all possible to get wisdom. Even when with knowledge, you cannot easily understand unless you have the understanding to help you unravel mysteries. Hence, understanding cannot come easy, except by wisdom. We can search all over the earth, at best, we shall get knowledge of all sorts of life's aspects. However, as I stated earlier, wisdom is required to unravel and make sense of the knowledge so acquired.

The Bible is notably and essentially a Book of Wisdom from God. Jesus Christ is clearly acclaimed as the Wisdom and Power of God in the Holy Scriptures. Even so, the Book of Proverbs is devoted to the wise sayings of Solomon, who sought God's Help to rule over God's people when he became the King after David, his father. The fear of God is the beginning of wisdom; the knowledge of the Holy One is understanding (Proverbs 9:10; Psalm 111;10).

God has described David as a man after His own Heart (1 Samuel 13:11-13). Yet, he fathered Solomon via a most horrendous, sinful exploit with his mother, Bathsheba (2 Samuel 11 and 12). Who would have imagined that God would still recommend King David to us as a man after His Own Heart? Who could have imagined that Bathsheba's son, Solomon would succeed King David? Okay, we can possibly agree that the Wisdom of God is a totally different matter from man's wisdom. God's Ways and Thoughts are Higher than man's even as the Heavens are far away from the earth, so are His Ways/Thoughts far away from ours (Isaiah 55:7-10).

The Fear of God is the Beginning of Wisdom...

The Holy Bible is very clear in its affirmation that the Fear of God is the beginning of Wisdom (Proverbs 1:7, 9:10; 111:10). The Book of Wisdom is a very wonderful exposition of this fact. All through the Holy Scriptures, this fact runs without relenting. So, if you know in your life that you need wisdom, or want to learn to fear God and be wise in His Name, look not elsewhere; not to the north, east, south or west, get the Word of God. It is no wonder that the Bible sells more than any other book in the world today and for a long many years before.

There are no short cuts to learning to fear God. You have to go through much sorrow and pain even as Jesus Christ Himself had to do on earth like us (Hebrews 5:7,8). You need a very strong desire for God and love for Him and value for Him, to want to learn His Ways. There will be many obstacles and troubles on the way (Psalm 34:17-19), but fear not Jesus said, for He has overcome this world (John 16:33) and all it has to offer. If you put your full trust in the Lord God in Jesus Christ and hope in Him entirely, you will make it and have good success in this endeavour.

Firstly, is to behold the essence of God as Love, Holy, Powerful beyond measure, Just and Fearsome. Awe-inspiring, full of Dread and is to be Dreaded absolutely for He is full with Awe. God is to be absolutely revered, hallowed as His Name too, above all other gods and above anything else (1 Chronicles 16:25;).

Our Lord Jesus Christ, who being of His very nature, God manifested in the flesh (John 1:1-15), lived to be both man and God. He had to experience what we must go through to return to God (from whom we all came in terms of having been created by Him, without whose spirit we cannot live, for His Breath is in us all regardless of our pride to or not to believe in His existence). He also had to be God for us to taste of God's reality in His Goodness, existing amongst us.

One of the foremost and greatest attributes of God is Love. For God so loved the world that He Gave His only Begotten Son, that whomsoever believes in Him should not perish but have everlasting life. All who do not believe stand condemned already (John 3:16-18). For all this love, God cannot love everybody and reserves the right to love as He Wills and not equally as humans think and or assume. God Spoke of Jesus Christ that He Is His Beloved Son, with whom He is well Pleased (Matthew 3:17; Mark 9:7; Luke 3:21-23). Not everybody can be so loved equally.

Jesus Christ chose twelve disciples and even they knew that John was the disciple whom Jesus loved (John 19:26; 21:7,20). Whenever He did special things or needed to be in special situations, Jesus Christ had with Him the Apostles Peter, James and John (sons of Zebedee), i.e. about two or three out of twelve disciples. God is not man and His Ways and Thoughts differ tremendously in an immeasurable way (Isaiah 55:7-9). So, beloved, be not deceived by the false teachings going round today about God loving all equally and unconditionally.

Like the WMD (Weapons of Mass Destruction) movement, the WWJD (what would Jesus do) movement is thriving as many other slogans-led movements that have no basis nor roots in the Word of God. They act as they know God above all else including God Himself. They postulate what God Would do or not as though God were speaking through them based upon their very human senses and sensibilities and imaginations.

What would Jesus do? How would anyone know, except to be very closely walking with Jesus Christ for the Holy Spirit to Guide and Lead them into all Truth and all Righteousness. Good works and all human kindness will get no one to Heaven. You can do all you can and give your whole life to charitable good works and perform too many miracles and healings etc. and yet go to hell (Matthew 7:22-24). God reveals Himself and His heart to those who fear Him.

The love for God is what draws anyone to learn to fear Him and get wise. Jesus Christ our Lord Himself attested to this great love in urging us to love the Lord our God with all our hearts too – and our souls, minds, bodies and everything we have (all our very beings) as a clear priority. This is a reflection of the very first three of the Ten Commandments (Deuteronomy 5). The Prophet Isaiah wrote prophetically that our Lord Jesus Christ delighted Himself in the Fear of God, thereby attesting to the utmost significance of fearing God.

Unlike so many who belittle the fear of God today and call those who teach the fear of God all sorts of names, the fear of God includes at its core, the fact that God Will Judge/Punish/Reward all as He deems fit. No one will escape the Judgement Seat of Jesus Christ. There is Divine Retribution for sin. God cannot be mocked (Galatians 6:7; 1Samuel 12:13-15) and we shall all reap whatever we have sown. I am amazed that people teach others that there is not a need to fear God and that God is all Love and thereby lead many into error. God's Word is so True and Accurate. Such teachers' judgement is already secured.

So, to learn to fear God is to love Him deeply and trust Him to His Word when He said He Will Punish disobedience severely and Reward and Bless obedience (Deuteronomy 28). This runs right through the Holy Scriptures and is not just an Old Testament "fad".

To fear God, we must be very seriously mindful also of His Power to punish sinfulness even unto eternal damnation. God hates sin. So, if anyone tells you that God loves you as you are and you know you are deeply steeped in sin, repent and know that what the Word of God says is that you have an opportunity to enter into the true love of God by forsaking sin, receiving forgiveness and following after the Way of God even according to the Teachings of the Commandments of God and Jesus Christ's exemplifying of Godly living on earth.

The fear of God is paramount to the rooting of anyone in the Christian Faith. Unfortunately, the fear of God is hardly effectively taught today. Hence, the fear of God is very scarcely in the hearts of men today. Rather, even new so-called believers are taught to the contrary, i.e. the need not to fear God. It has become a very unpopular thing to teach the fear of God and thus we hear of a God who is all loving and this supposedly, regardless of sin. This is far from the Reality and Truth of God even in Jesus Christ.

We can observe a clear disregard for God and or His punitive ability with regard to judging sinful behaviour and wilful disobedience to God's Laws and Commandments in so-called believers today.

Jesus Christ made clear that He Came to fulfil and not condemn the Law (Matthew 5:17). Furthermore, the proof of willingness to subject oneself fully to God is to be absolutely determined to obey His Commandments and Word regardless of what any man may think of one. Jesus Christ emphasized this Truth as did all the Inspired writers of the Holy Word of God in the Scriptures – to fear God and obey His Commandments.

The fear of God will Root any keen sincere follower or seeker after God in Jesus Christ to the Way, Truth and Life. This is the core requirement of the Christian Faith/Walk. To fear and obey God is to show proof that one loves God truly. The pledge of a new conscience to God in dying to the old sinful self and being renewed in mind soul body heart and all is essentially being born again of the Spirit and of Water (is to be baptised into God the Father, Son and Holy Spirit). When you come to believe, you must prove your faith (1 Peter 1:6-8; Acts 26:20; 1 Corinthians 4:2).

This disposition is Rewarded by God as Jesus Christ Himself said that when we show proof of such love for Him in obeying His Commandments, He and the Father will come and make home with such a person. What a Great impetus for me to strive daily to be perfect/holy (1 Peter 1:16; Matthew 5:48) as God requires of us in the Holy Scriptures. Not that I have attained unto this yet, but I choose to strive to be. This is and must be the choice of any true believer.

Rather than presenting the fear of God to people as though our Loving God is a terrorist type of uncaring person or even animal as some do today and many actually say to their shame, God urges us to choose Him of our own free will. God wants us to opt for Him in thoughts, words and deeds; wholesomely, in fearful obedience and loving devotion. I urge you therefore to choose God (Deuteronomy 30:19).

This must be guided by faithful hope that works through love (Galatians 5:6); that we would please Him in so doing and attain unto Eternal life as a result. This is not because we deserve so much Love, Blessing and Grace at all; rather, that God truly does Love us and wants for us to draw near to Him willingly so He can Draw near to us. When God comes near to anyone, Blessings, Mercy, Grace and Love Will Flow freely.

The Bible makes very clear that the angels of God encamp around those who fear Him and tremble at His every word (Psalm 34:7; Isaiah 66:2). There are those who dare to believe and follow (keep to) His Standard as set out to Guide us in His Word. So, to follow popular culture of disobedience is to wilfully disobey God. Jesus Christ likened obedience to His Word by His hearers to one building his house upon the rocks so that when the storms rage, the house stands and is not destroyed (Luke 6:47-49).

On the other hand, the house of the disobedient is built upon the sand and cannot withstand the harsh reality of raging storms (and attending great floods) whose power overwhelms the house on the sand and it gets washed sadly away. So, we do have a choice. Do we want our house to be able to withstand the test of the raging storms or washed away and perish? The only way to have the former is to obey God's Word and that latter is the result of disobedience.

I strongly urge my reader and anyone who genuinely wants to stand the test of time and pass through the Judgement Seat successfully and receive the Crown of Life that will never fade away, to reflect on their lives and check for the direction they are headed towards right now; for, it may be too late tomorrow. Please bear in mind that it is not my wish to prove that I am better than anyone at all; but the love of God compels me to obey Him in delivering this message to the world.

Today is yours as yesterday was. You do not know whether you will see the end of today; nor do you know that you will see tomorrow. We are encouraged in the Word of God to live each day as though it were our last. Beloved, are you ready to face the Judgement Seat of Jesus Christ if death came knocking today? You alone know.

Learning to Fear God...

As I wrote earlier and repeat over and over in one form or another only to drum this message in, our Lord Jesus Christ delighted Himself in the fear of God (Hebrews 5:7-10). He considered this superior (Isaiah 11:3) to all other things, of all gifts and all else that God Endowed Him with. Surely, our Lord Jesus Christ learnt obedience through the things He suffered. That the fear of God is the beginning of Wisdom is not a matter of/for questioning. It is a fact of the faith walk. Faith of course is being sure of what you hope for and certain of what you have not seen (Hebrews 11:1). With faith, you just believe.

Some say that is stupid, foolish, unrealistic, nonsensical, not credible etc. Well, okay, you must choose for yourself. However, what is stupid, foolish, even crazy to man, is the beginning of God's Wisdom. Whether you believe in God or not is irrelevant to the reality of God. What if you are wrong and there is a God? Can you come back to life after you have died to make amends? No. So, my dear reader, be wise. Do we not say in general terms, in common language, that it is better to be safe than sorry? You must choose.

God is the Great I AM (Exodus 3:14). God is without beginning nor end; yet, God is the Alpha and Omega; the beginning and the end (Revelation 21:6; 22:13). So much so, as Jesus Christ Himself is God, He is the Author and Finisher of our (the) Faith. So, when Jesus Christ begins a work, if you are wise, faithful, willing and obedient, you must just believe (and fully trustingly) that He who began the good work in/for you is more than Able to complete/finish it even until the Day of our Lord Jesus Christ (Philippians 1:6). Amen. The Bible says that I know in whom I have believed and I am persuaded that He is Able to keep that which I have committed unto Him until that Day (2 Timothy 1:12).

What is it that I have committed unto Him? My everything – my life, will, body, soul, spirit, mind, time, heart, being – and yes totally – when I received Him into my life and forgiveness was Granted unto me through undeserved Mercy and such Grace. Since Jesus Christ came into my life, He Took over and has done a Better work in me than my parents, family, friends, peers, drugs, make-up, etc. could ever achieve. I willingly give up the world and all to follow Him without looking back ever; so Help me Father in the Name of my Lord Jesus. Amen.

If you cannot fear God, there is no way you can willingly obey His Commandments. Sin is very sweet and when man knows and or thinks that he will not be punished for sin, he will run and always runs riot. Even when man knows for sure, it is hard to obey.

It is very hard for man to follow God's Ways in his flesh; this is why there is a need to fear God. The fear of God combined with the choice (willingness) to obey God will Enable the Holy Spirit of God to Come and make living for God easier for the believer to bear. Discipline has and will never be easy (Hebrews 12:5-11).

Our Lord Jesus Christ exemplified the Perfect God in man; both as man and as God. He learnt obedience through the things he suffered. It could never have been easy. He delighted Himself in the fear of God. He willingly rejected the world when satan offered despite the attractions the world held (Luke 1:4-13). He chose to obey even unto the crucifixion through the pain and all the sorrows and anguish. For which reason God Exalted Him above all else in Heaven and on earth – that at the Name of Jesus, every knee must bow and every tongue confess that Jesus Christ is Lord (Philippians 2:9-11).

Jesus Christ being therefore God, Son of God, Son of Man (God being the original Man for He created us in His image), Jesus Christ did not need to fear God. Jesus Christ displayed the awesome

Power of God visibly, like no ordinary man or human (before or after) with such ease and such Authority. Yet, He delighted Himself in the fear of God. Not that God needs us to fear Him; but to show us how to reach His Heart.

We have this gracious opportunity to fear Him and obey His Commandments here on earth whilst we still have life. It is only now that you can honour God, dear reader. This is impossible from the grave. Whatever decision you do choose to make, remember that now is the time and chance you do have. When death comes (and it will surely come) no one will be able to say no; and it will be final, next would come Judgement (Hebrews 9:27). I urge you to be wise and choose to learn to fear God all the days of your life on this earth.

The modern, "psychedelic", exposition of Christianity cannot be accurate at all. It is devoid of the fear of God – evidenced by the extent of decadence, attending wilful laxity of morality and disobedience, apparent display of reprobate mindsets etc. in the behaviour of a vast majority of those who claim to be born again Christians. We make all sorts of excuses for not living holy.

A recent study asked people why they don't attend for church meetings etc. The result amazed many; and even I find it very interesting indeed (and I am sure many others too). As I knelt beside my bed meditating upon God's Word and listened to a discussion on a famous Christian radio station in England, I heard the discussion. I had essentially concluded my message when I came to access this information.

The respondents to the survey largely proffered that their decision for non-church attendance etc. was based on the unrealistic way in which God is presented to people in this modern times as a mediocre type of god who is supposed to hate sin and yet condones sin and does not punish for sin as expected. Such a loving god with such unconditional love who loves you anyway however you are and regardless of your sinfulness made no sense they said.

They said perhaps if God were to be presented the traditional way; as the awesome, mighty God, worthy to be feared, praised and adored, revered, hallowed; that punishes sin and rewards holy and righteous living, then God will become more alive for people to come in search of again. That should bring back the reality of God again for humans to deal with. There is a sure reason for revival.

The presentation of God as your friend to talk to as any other human being creates the impression in people that you do not need to fear God; and I have heard many popular preachers preach this falsehood to their shame and the potential destruction of many people's faith.

They say to the people that friends are not to be feared but approached simply, with equality and openness etc. thereby equating God with man? Great shame indeed. May God Arise and scatter His enemies in this day and age for His Glory. Amen. Jesus Christ, being God, did not usurp God's Authority in showing us the Way. Rather, he humbled Himself (Philippians 2:5-7) even unto the most humiliating death in crucifixion.

The fear of God is real and must be taught by those whom the Lord has Called to do so. Even though many are called, few are chosen; of the chosen, like Israel, are the most stubborn and God Knows this. Yet, it is a terrible thing for anyone to fall under the wrath of God. Faith comes by hearing the Word of God (Romans 10:17). The Bible says how can the hearer(s) know of a God they have not heard of and cannot see and have not met? Unless of course they are preached to and taught about Him? How can the preachers etc. do their bit unless they have been Sent?

The decadence we see today only serves to confirm that many out there claiming to be of the Lord have not been Sent by God.

They are causing the destruction of many. Those who ought to be destroyed are being spared at the expense of those who ought to be spared (Ezekiel 13:19). Jesus Himself warns us in His Word that many call His Name and call Him Lord, Lord etc. but their hearts are far from Him. There are many impostors at large and the true believers must guard their spirits, lest they be deceived.

I very strongly urge my readers to search after the Ancient of Days. Our great and mighty God in Jesus Christ; He was, is and is to come. Forever He Will Be. He Lives forever and ever. Amen.

Did not Jesus Christ Himself declare that before Abraham was (John 8:58), He Is? Beloved, let the fear of God become rooted and entrenched in your heart. Then God will really come alive in your life so you can come into the Knowledge of God in spirit and in truth. Revelation only comes to any one from God through God's Wisdom. According to the Word of God, Solomon was anointed King of God's people and He knew He needed wisdom and went humbly to God (2 Chronicles 1:7-12).

God Blessed King Solomon as requested and much more for He Was Pleased that the King's request was humble and focused. God Blessed Him with so much and he eventually allowed this to get into his head to his shame. With wisdom like no one before or after him and wealth and power at his disposal, rather than stick very closely to the fear of God (which spared David) and allow all his ways to be guided accordingly, he strayed. Yet, he left an account of his walk with God in the gift of God to him in wisdom; so much, for us to learn from when we want to follow God.

The wisdom of God will change any life for the better. My dear reader, pray unto the Father of all Lights in Jesus Christ's Holy Name and pledge a good conscience unto God to live a life worthy of Him and God may just honour you with an Answer that will change your life forever unto eternal life.

Practicalities of Fearing God...

To fear God is to be wary that God Will fulfil His Warning/Promise to Bless obedience and Punish disobedience. This is to say that God Will Do what He Says He Will Do. Let me site the example of parenting a child. Often, a parent would set guiding rules for the child and threaten to punish disobedience and not fulfil this threat when the child disobeys. The child tests and retests; if there is still no effective fulfilment of the parents' word, then there is a loss of respect for the parents' word. The child then needs not fear punishment for any disobedient behaviour.

Likewise, with God, to fear God is to know beyond any doubts whatsoever that God's Word Will be fulfilled. To fear God is to fully and absolutely trust and obey His Word and Himself. To fear God is to believe that you will be Blessed for your obedience and you stand accursed for your disobedience. The fear of God will therefore keep the believer in check over attitudes and behavioural trends, as well as what God's expectations are in the Faith walk for all who believe. The person who fears God will diligently learn God's Word and put same to practice and teach others by living as an example. Such a person will care more to obey God than yield to man's ridicule.

The fear of God takes root in and from the very things that many now discard as archaic, unnecessary and irrelevant in the faith walk. Propriety in worship (1 Corinthians 11:1-16) is a vital example of how God is supposed to be honoured. The Apostle Paul taught a lot about this which is now regarded as unreasonable, inappropriate and only written for some archaic macho culture(s). What a lie from the pits of hell. These same perverts of God's Word do not say the same of tithes and they give prosperity acclaim that fills their lives and their listeners' desires today.

The fear of God is rooted in little steps of obedience in honour of God and His Word through propriety in worship, even as the believer obeys the Commandments of God and in a humble disposition in approaching God. God hates arrogance (James 4:6; 1 Peter 5:5). Yet, many are even encouraged to approach God with gross rudeness, in the name of a fake kind of assertion, especially when humans want for something, as if God must answer to our needs. We now freely command God as if to make Him do our bidding in the same way as we manipulate each other for the sake of taking advantage of the weak and or to bully the stronger or those in authority over us.

It is no wonder why many are languishing away in our congregations, fellowships and so called churches in abject poverty of spirit and lacking in even basic provisions that are freely available to people in the world, who watch us and judge God.

They adjudge (albeit wrongly) that our God manifests in "us" as we gather more or less in vain. We thereby dishonour the Holy Name through our disobedience and lack of fear for God and the taking of His Name in vain. We use more slangs and make-up, even more than the "world" in our gatherings. Language that would make even some in the world shriek in disgust we use freely on our pulpits. Does this change God? No. God has reserved a remnant (Ezra 9:8; Isaiah 10:21; Micah 5:8; Romans 9:27, 11:8) who will surely bring Glory to His Holy Name.

We bow to God; not necessarily just in our hearts being absolutely humble, but in learning to kneel, prostrate, bow etc. in His Presence when we pray. It is not appropriate to clothe ourselves in unrighteousness and or worldliness (1 Timothy 2; 1 Peter 3; Colossians 3) and come to God in the glory of this world.

The Word of God is very clear on this matter. Yet, as if we are to make our own word to obey, so called leaders of so called churches continue after their own imaginations. The Word of God says that we must not lean upon our own understanding. This very thing we do increasingly. Well, the Lord is not pleased at all and if no one will go in His Name, I choose to be one of those who will. There are several ways in which we dishonour God's Word. I will lay out an example.

A very good example (now condemned and controversial) is the issue of head covering for women and none for men. This is very clearly laid out in the Holy Scriptures. Yet, the amount of controversial and ridiculous debates around this particular issue is phenomenal. Another issue is the woman's role within the Church, also well laid out in the Holy Scriptures, especially not to teach or usurp authority over men (1 Timothy 2:12).

The equality and feminist movements have skilfully drafted in their practitioners to manipulate the Word of God and because of our love for sin and disobedience, we bought into these worldly teachings, hook, line and sinker, to our shame. We have exchanged the Glory of our Living God for the opposite, the glory of this world; and we bear full responsibility daily for our actions.

By so doing, we follow satan's wiles like our fathers and mothers before us. First we allowed the equality of women with men issue to enter, in support of the moral laxity and heavy sexual immorality within our members. Once this entered, it has deeply opened up other issues that came tumbling down; and we think God can be pleased with us? We prophesy out of our own minds and rather than be filled with the Holy Spirit, we are filled with wines and various alcoholic drinks (spirits) which multiply the demonic spirits amongst us very fast.

The Apostle Paul made very clear in his letter to the Corinthians that a woman must cover her head when praying or prophesying because of the angels. Angels of course are the ministering spirits of the Living God. Likewise men ought not to cover their heads.

Any God fearing man or woman will dread to disobey and thus dishonour God's Word. To hear the various interpretations is just unreal. Some say that the covering the Apostle was talking about is the woman's hair and thus women are encouraged to do whatever idolatry with their hair (heads).

We are very clever indeed and can fabricate excuses faster than the speed of light if that were possible, since we have this great working brain and a choice. However, God's Word is very clear. We are sharper, better and more convincing than some magicians. However, God's Word prevails and remains unshakeable forevermore.

Gradually, these satanists and God haters pushed hard on the issue of women and men wearing each other's clothes, knowing fully well for example that a woman in men's clothes takes a different form entirely in body-flaunting etc. Many are fearful to preach against these matters and when you look into what is called church today, we see the world at large. Who's fooling who? Can we fool God? No way.

There is blatant disobedience against God's Word and not only is sexual immorality freely flowing in the so called churches; it is condoned, encouraged and practised by the elders/leaders of these congregations and their wives and children. Yet, we genuinely feel that God is pleased. Does this demonstrate a fear of/for God? I say not.

Before a man (even one truly called) takes up his cross, his wife attacks him for being crazy or mad and insists that God is not a man to care about these "little" things. It has become a very rare thing to find a man whose wife submits to him in obedience to God's Word. There are all sorts of excuses tendered. Of course as the Prophet Jeremiah wrote as Inspired by God, the women said that their husbands were there and saw them when they baked bread and cakes to the queen of heaven (Jeremiah 44:19) etc. what did the men do?

As with Adam and Eve, men have failed in their Godly responsibility and it is now very rare to find a man of God. The Teacher told us in Ecclesiastes indeed that out of a thousand people, He found only one righteous man and no woman at all amongst them (Ecclesiastes 7:28). What has changed today? I say not a lot if anything at all; things are much worse and surely as it was in the days of Noah, Jesus said so shall it be when the Son of Man shall return (Luke 17:26) as He Promised long ago. Well, be prepared.

How many men have been driven out of home especially in so-called developed countries, where men have been rendered impotent, because men refuse to stand for what is righteous. Men do not want the responsibility and discipline that goes with it. For a bowl of porridge, a man will forsake God not to talk of a bit of sex (in or out of marriage). What a shame. We love and lust after sex and worship our women and wives rather than worship the Great God. Many of us are so warped that we are on heat any and everywhere even in front of the children and we think nothing of it. No wonder incest is on the increase.

Naturally, we hear more of offences committed by men against women sexually and physically than those committed by women against men. I have studied long and hard over so many years and found that whether you want to believe it or not, men are as harassed by women as women by men. The "nature" of the woman is such that the whole world is programmed to treat the woman with less harshness. This is reflected in society everywhere. In prisons, mental institutions, etc. men are over-represented freely. What I am saying here is that our lives have become so very distorted basically because of the lack of the fear of God in our hearts and lives. More than ever before we need God. We need to change our ways lest we perish forever.

Well, it is very easy in a man-hating society to drive men out of home freely. Women are then free to do as they please in disobedience to God's Word. Both men and women are guilty; but what is essential for those willing to follow the Way of God and walk in the fear of God is to find out what the Word of God says and live by the Word of God. This is what prolongs life.

A prominent woman television executive on one of the Christian channels began to touch on this matter. I took notes. She went almost too deep and against the protocol of political correctness to the visible discomfort of her husband beside her. She did not stop except short of exposing herself personally in a direct way. She ended up doing so in saying she is also guilty like many (of being probably more worldly and increasingly so, than the women of the world). She also amazingly emphasized "especially us women" on live television. However, for many men, it is a taboo area especially when their wives are barely managing to stay with them at home.

Eve is as clever as ever. This has been continuously attested to by many women and girls and ladies I have ministered to personally over many years, regardless of the "advancement" man claims. I have heard preachers go on as if proud of their wives' and daughters' exploits over them at home daily.

They know quite well that their wives and daughters are "working" them and these "men of God" fall for it all the time deliberately. Not many men have the guts to be men anymore and a lot of men are very unmanly to the distaste of the women who want to eat their cakes as usual and have it still. Whilst these men encourage and reward what is clearly inappropriate and manipulative behaviour at home, they preach something to the congregations that they want to hear and not necessarily God's Word at all.

Well sir, know that like Adam, God will Judge you. Madam, know that like Eve, God will Judge you. Children, know that like the children of Israel, you also will face God's Judgement likewise. As surely as the devil has already received his Judgement, we all shall be judged.

Oh don't get me wrong at all. I am not saying that I am perfect but I am obeying God for this generation so that no one will say no one told them. I am not writing to please man or woman or child, only to please God who Sent me and to obey Him. I urge you to fear God. You who know that God has called you and spoken to you in the light of what you are reading, what are you waiting for? What are you frightened of? God Will ask of you what you did with His Counsel; be assured of this. If you do not obey, God will find another.

Fear God and obey His Commandments. Get rid of the jezebel spirit and do not encourage her. Forsake your love for jezebel and her charms sewn on her hands and her jewels and fine oils and perfumes and quest for power. Forsake all your love for worldliness and all it has to offer and follow after the Heart of God like David and let the Word of God enter and work within your members to honour the Holy God. Forsake your idols and the idolatrous ways of your forefathers before you. Fear God I charge you in Jesus' Name. Amen.

Better to breakdown the house now and re-lay a new foundation in the Name of Jesus Christ, based on correct standards of rooting; not political correctness. Otherwise, it will be too late, as predicted, even by Jesus Christ Himself. As it was in the days of Noah, so shall it be when the Son of Man shall come. Will He find faith on the earth? Will Jesus Christ find you faithful to His Word?

Now is our chance to judge ourselves and test ourselves and see if we are truly in the faith or not. You can judge me as harshly as you like, but should you find in the Word of God that I am right, will you have the same determination to change your ways and obey God? Isaiah the Prophet heard the Voice of the Lord Calling out saying who will go in the Name of the Lord and he said here I am

Lord, Send me. Will you be ready to go in the Name of the Lord? Time is short.

No Halfway...

My brethren, beloved, there is no short cut to the Kingdom of God, no half ways, no half measures to being rooted in the Word of God. God hates standing on the fence which many of you love to do. Likened unto being hot or cold, Jesus will spit out those who are lukewarm (Revelation 3:16). God wants us to be clear with Him. We are either for or against Him. We must be hot or cold. God said in the Book of Revelation that He would spit out the lukewarm from His mouth. But I am writing about my Father's business. Better to take a stand for or against God.

Jesus Christ said anyone who is not against us is for us (Mark 9:38-41). This is only saying that anyone who will not work against the interests of the Lord Jesus Christ or His Followers is in a way pro-Jesus; as such people cannot be considered a danger or hindrance to Jesus Christ's message. However, it is evident that anyone who is proactively engaged in hindering the message is against Jesus Christ's interests.

You are with God if you are diligently seeking to learn more of Him and you put to practice what He Teaches and or Commands, Instructs, for His Followers to do and or not to do. No matter how well educated you are and how excellently skilled you are (in several ways), if you cannot obey God's Word, you are not of Him.

If you must argue and make excuses and put your own personal interpretations and twists on His Words, you cannot be His disciple. Many deceive themselves; not wanting to be seen as troublemakers, we readily compromise the Word of God. We want the world to like us. We do not want to be hated and or persecuted. We love the one-leg-in-and-one-leg-out approach and we readily quote Scriptures to back up our falsehoods, thereby making a non-sense of the Word of God, which is Holy.

When it suits us, we are with the world and go out of our way to outdo Hollywood (the epitome of the world) and its attendant culture in practically every way. We outdo them and even invoke their envy in their tummy tucks, makeovers, dress code of a very sensual nature, etc.; in thoughts, words and deeds too. We then come together on Sundays or whenever we choose and weep and wail and trample the courts of wherever we claim to worship a God that we refuse to obey.

No wonder the Prophet wrote that God hates all this noise and trampling of His Courts (Isaiah 1:11-13). We have become an offence unto His Nostrils rather than a sweet aroma in holy offerings of our praises. Let all men lift up holy hands is what the Lord requires not worldly hands.

We do these things totally devoid and oblivious of the Standard of God to fear Him, witness to His Power and Great and Mighty Deeds and obey His Commandments. Thereby not encouraging others to fear and come to Him for salvation through reconciliation (2 Corinthians 5:11-21) via Jesus Christ our Lord. Like our fathers before us, we condemn and malign and persecute and seek to destroy whatever and whomsoever will dare to make themselves available unto God for the sake of the Holy and Righteous Word/Gospel day to day.

We readily attest to the chief priests and Pharisees etc., with regard to the killing our Lord Jesus Christ; and we, just like them, are quickest to condemn and persecute all who stand firm for the Truth – just as it is written. Rather than nurture and promote the fear of God, we fear man and his laws. The Bible makes clear that woe be unto and upon all who make unjust laws (Isaiah 10:1). Yet, the nations readily are changing all the laws that were put in place and formed after the Guidance of the Holy Scriptures.

We who claim to be of God and in Christ Jesus seek to get "serious" with calling God only when we are in trouble with the world and the world with us seek for God only when events like 911 happen as in the case of New York, United States of America; or as in the world wars. So, God does allow us to trap ourselves into seeking for Him.

We then blame God and ask foolish and irresponsible questions like where was God when these things were happening? As if whenever God says do not do this or that, we would stop and not do it. We have His Laws and Commandments and we choose to satisfy our own whims and caprices anyway; and we even quote His Word in fake self comfort when we engage in evil. Even when God manifestly comes to our aid, we take the Glory for and unto ourselves. We fail to honour Him as the faithful did in the past. We take His Name in vain and or in blasphemous arrogance.

We are quick to invoke and mention His Holy Name when we want to impress others; and we are masters at the game of impressing one another. We have excellent gifts from this Great and Wonderful God; but we use the gifting, not to Bless His Holy Name, but to create fun and fiestas for ourselves and for the consumption of our lustful appetites; all to our vane delights and shameful lusting after evil ways. We quite happily use God's Name when we want others to fear us; and to avoid the wrath of God, when we are in conflict with the world.

Hence, we drag the Name of our Holy God in the mud and cause the world not only to do so but also to hate any association(s) with the Name of our God, even Jesus Christ.

Who do we fool and for how long? If God hates for us to be lukewarm and will spit such out of His Mouth on that Day of Judgement, let no one be deceived; for whether you believe, obey or not, God cannot be mocked. We shall all reap whatever we sow. If you sow your seed unto the sinful nature, of that nature you shall reap; and if onto the spirit of truth, of that too you shall reap (Galatians 6:7-9). God is Just.

I urge you beloved with my whole heart and being to very strongly consider and take a stand today. If for Jesus Christ, be clear and go all the way; if for satan, likewise. At least you know that your fate is in your own hands through the power of your choice given to you by this Holy and Just God. You only have yourself to blame if you are on the path of destruction. As the Bible says, there is a way that seems right to a man, in the end it leads to death (Proverbs 14:12). Your decision is made by your choice.

I strongly and lovingly urge you though to choose the narrow path (Matthew 7:13-15) and thereby choose God in Jesus Christ, the Ancient of Days, in whose Name alone is there Salvation, first for the Jews, then for the gentiles. There is no other Name (Acts 4:12) given by which we can be saved through reconciliation with the Holy God, our God, even Christ Jesus for the salvation of our souls. Thank You Jesus. Amen.

Profitable Boldness and Loss...

In a nutshell, to be halfway is really to opt for satan, the master of half truths (equivalent only to lies and falsehoods). God will not have that. So, I urge you to understand that there is absolutely no point in being a false, gentle person at all. Rather, be bold. Beloved, do not waste your gifts and talents if you are bold. There is no profit in engaging boldly in what does not save. There is no use in boldly fighting a lost battle that leads only to death. In death, there is no redemption.

Let me remind those of you my readers who are acquainted with the Way (the Word of God) that ever since the time of John the Baptist, the Kingdom of God has been forcefully advancing and the forceful men take hold of it (Matthew 11:12). You cannot be less than bold and expect to achieve the goal of learning the fear of God and His Way of Faithful Love. You cannot afford to be fearful; for God did not give you a spirit of timidity but one of Power, Love and a sound mind in the Holy Spirit (Romans 8:14-16).

I will also bring to your attention and or remembrance, or at least a fresh insight to your hearing, that fear is as a sin unto God. There is no room for the fearful in the Kingdom of God. The fearful shall not inherit the Kingdom of God (Revelation 21:8), which is for the bold. So, all our lives must be given unto God in full, maximum trust.

Have you observed the way of a child? So pure and so very innocent; yet, so real and so very admirable. This of course before pollution and or corruption by family and or larger societal influences. Jesus Christ recommended, in fact, declared that anyone who cannot and or does not come (and or accept the Word of God) as a little child cannot inherit the Kingdom of Heaven, the Kingdom of God (Matthew 18:2-4).

The Kingdom of God is not for the so-called learned, wise, old, enlightened ones at all. Jesus declared to His disciples privately that they should rejoice that they see and hear what they see and hear. For many of old (kings and priests etc.) prayed to see and hear what they see and hear but could not. Jesus also enthused unto them that these things are revealed to little children (Luke 10:21) and hidden from the wise and learned. God is all wise and the student of profitable boldness must seek God for the Wisdom to understand why God's Ways are so different. Remember again, the fear of God is the beginning of wisdom.

The Kingdom of God is not revealed unto the rich and powerful as a matter of course either. It is for the humble, poor, destitute, despised and rejected. As we see in the Holy Scriptures, although born a King, Jesus Christ was born a commoner, in a manger, into a humble family.

Contrary to today's norm in our societies, such a humble beginning was no excuse for failure to follow through with our Lord's Destiny. Jesus Christ showed a remarkable example of boldness in the face of the harsh realities of being hated without any reason at all. Jesus Christ declared the Word of God with power (and very boldly) with regard to the Kingdom of God; and at the relevant times, publicly too. He declared likewise, His Oneness with Almighty God, with Power to Send the Holy Spirit. In due season, the Holy Spirit was indeed sent. Amen. Halleluyah.

Jesus Christ said no one has seen the Father except (Him of course) the One who came from the Father. No one knows the Father or Son except whom the Father or Son Revealed Him unto. Whomsoever has seen the Son has seen the Father (John 14:7-9). Yet so humble and so meek, the boldness of Jesus Christ cannot be overemphasised. Or shall we take the example of Abraham, referred to as God's friend (James 2:23). Moses, accredited with being the most humble man that ever lived. He dealt with Pharaoh effectively in due season. Many examples can be given.

Let me try Joshua, who took over from Moses, to lead Israel to the Promised Land. Uneasy lies the head that wears the crown.

Let us remember that Solomon prayed especially for Wisdom. He prayed to God; he did not go to the so-called wise men and or women in the land at all. He humbled himself and went on his knees. Humbled his heart. That takes boldness and maturity and is a profitable type of boldness.

Solomon took time out of the powerful position he found himself in to sincerely seek out the Lord for His Wisdom to deal with his new role, leading the Israel of God at that material time. So did Joshua as Moses before him.

Gideon, like them too, was the most unlikely candidate for leadership in his family. He was however chosen by God for an arduous task. He came clean with God with reverent fear and humility that he was not at all worthy. Yet he was bold enough to ask God for a sign (Judges 6:16-18) that God will see him through.

This is the type of humble boldness, like the Lion of Judah, that is required, to follow God in Jesus Christ with fearful, humble, transparency of intent, that greatly pleases God. There is a very childlike simplicity about such boldness, which makes the average child loveable mostly to all. God Will always honour and keep His Covenant of love (Deuteronomy 7:9) with all who demonstrate such attributes as these. Such people will not fail to attract God's attention.

God's Holy Spirit searches (Proverbs 27:20; Revelations 2:23; 1 Chronicles 28:9) out the whole earth and hearts of mankind for those who truly fear and love Him. To such, God avails Himself and

Blesses them with a righteousness not of their own making for the surety of living a life pleasing to God.

Let me give the example of the harlot Rahab (Joshua 2) who helped the children of Israel to hide those sent to spy out the land promised to them. In due season, she was singled out for Blessing. God Touched her surely and I can postulate that she never continued in that horrible trade after her encounter with God. When some use this experience in preaching today, they make out like it is pleasing to God for a person to engage in prostitution. The way they present it is what I am referring to here and not the experience, as though a change is not absolutely required.

I encourage you who may be in prostitution at this time male or female and those in the bondage of homosexual and lesbian behaviour as well as those in adultery, witchcraft, wizardry, sorcery of all sorts and thieving lying, whatever has mastered you, take heart. Be bold and willing to change. Submit to the Master, Jesus Christ and receive His Holy Breath even right now. I ask the Father in Jesus' Name to break whatever has taken an unholy hold over you. Amen.

The Prophet Malachi wrote as he was Inspired of God to write of such people who fear God and met together in his short book for the records in the Holy Scriptures. There is written of such people a reward from God that is special. You need to go and read that book (Malachi 3) meditatively in prayer to behold the reward for such profitable boldness and the loss incurred in not following after that Way.

I am strongly urging that this devoted commitment to humbly, mournfully seek the Lord in worship and prayer continuously be your hearts desire; as it is what profits in the long run of the faith journey. We are running a race and not all shall win. So, we need to run according to the rules and or standards set (2 Timothy 2:5). Although not all can take the lead or win, all have the chance to finish the race. Although, if you do not run according to the rules, even though you reach the end, you will be disqualified as though you did not finish.

So, beloved, be sure you are running according to the rules. This is only a warning as I am called to sound the trumpet; you have been warned. Paul the Apostle said he preaches to himself (1 Corinthians 9:27) after preaching to others publicly or otherwise; and for one reason only, that he should not find that after such hard work, he should lose the prize. It would be a dire and sheer loss to start and lose out.

One will be disqualified due to not following through by diligently obeying the rules. For example, for not sticking to one's lane in a race. Even if one finishes, for crossing lanes, disqualification means total loss, as good as running for nothing. This is good for nothing, absolute loss, a futile effort, a chasing after the winds or shadows.

On the other hand however, it is profitable to boldly take on the challenge systematically; first to prepare; fully studying the rules of the race and presenting for the start with a clear goal – to finish and be counted amongst those who finish honourably. In the case of the Christian walk, we strive to finish with those who will attain unto the Kingdom of God and receive the Crown of Life that will never fade away (James 1:12).

What does it profit a man to lose his soul and gain this whole world (Matthew 16:26). When you die it is finished. What do you gain from all your vanity when you know that your secrets will be revealed in the Light when the Time comes and that Time will surely come.

Should you perish because you are so stubborn and will not accept the truth because it is bitter. You can hate me but do not hate the truth. Persecute me by all means but save your soul. At the end of the day, I want my Crown of Life. This is my objective. What is yours? Finery? Wealth? The choice is indeed yours. However, I urge you to seek first the Kingdom of God and His Righteousness, then all things shall be added unto you according to the Will of God.

Of Race and Purpose...

So, my dear reader, are you running the race? Do you know that whether you are conscious of it or not you have already been registered for this race (Galatians 2:2, 5:7) the moment you came into this world? The Bible says that it is appointed for mankind, once to die and after that Judgement (Hebrews 9:27). If you do not run you will still be judged as not having finished anyway.

So, whilst you have the life force in you, better to make ready for the race. Start now, not later. So you think it is too late? No you are not late yet, not for this race. Jesus said about this race that the first shall be the last and the last shall be the first (Matthew 19:30, 20:16).

This race is a Spiritual one. What will be your goal then for this race? What will you be trying to achieve? Some live life for various reasons. Whilst some live for satan, some choose God. Some live and will sell their souls to the devil just to be famous; some will give all up for Jesus Christ and the Gospel Message.

Many take decisions without thinking of the end, which justifies the means or vice-versa. If you run, you will need a goal anyway. If you do not run you will still be judged. So, I strongly urge you to run and be very prepared and have a goal. The race we are running is a very different one than the worldly chop-and-let-chop dog-eat-dog one – rat-race style. Chop means to eat, take my share/turn.

The real race I am writing about is the race for Eternal Life in Christ Jesus which begins with being born again (John 3:3,7,16-18) by first of all accepting Jesus Christ's Sacrifice as True and Real and yielding your life unto Jesus Christ for His Direction and Leading by His Holy Spirit into all Truth and all Righteousness. This is the only race that matters ultimately. This is the race for the Kingdom of God which Jesus Christ strongly Counselled that we take the Narrow Road (Matthew 7:12-15) to enter therein.

The worldly race is for worldly acclaim and trophies and glories that will be eaten up by moth and rust and will perish. There is no reward. It is without profit; a complete loss. The Heavenly race for the Kingdom of God is that which will deliver the Crown of Life that will never fade away (1 Peter 5:4). At best the worldly race will lead to death and eternal damnation. For this reason, I strongly urge you to have a goal and be sure that this is the one you want; for it is for this that your labour shall be targeted – ultimately, in vain or for gain.

The Bible says that God's people perish because of a lack of a vision (Proverbs 29:18). So, it is expedient that we set our eyes and focus on Jesus Christ (Hebrews 12:2), the Author and Finisher of our Faith and of life itself. Jesus Christ is the Alpha and Omega, beginning and end (Revelation 1:8; 22:13). Only Jesus can give us a profitable vision and sustain our drive to reach the targeted goal.

Only Jesus Christ can be with us as we run the race when we have Heaven (the Kingdom of God) as our goal; and of course only satan can do likewise when we choose the worldly race. Be assured that only Jesus Christ can lead us to the profitable end; right from giving the profitable vision, through to sustaining us in the running, to keep us on track, to the very end where He would Deliver the Crown unto all who stand firm to the very end (Matthew 10:22; Mark 13:13), with their eyes kept focused all the time on Him, our Source and Resource and Life, Jesus Christ our Lord, Amen.

Your race and purpose can only make any sense if they are synonymous with one another. It is no use running a race for the Kingdom of God with a worldly purpose/goal; or for the world with a Godly goal/purpose. That will conflict right through to no godly, spiritual, conclusive end.

Many notable so-called leaders of the Faith teach that you cannot live a Godly life that Jesus expects of you and so lead others astray (and they give up) and say that we are now only under grace, so sin increases amongst us and within our members. Yet, the discipline to submit to the Holy Spirit remains available for those who want Truth, to Enable the Faithful to live a holy life in Jesus Christ. Be not deceived. You can live a holy life with the Help of the Holy Spirit. Do not be misled.

Of the Kingdom of God and the world...

What would it profit you to gain the whole world and lose your soul anyway? You can have all you want in life like King Solomon. Have you read about him in the Bible (2 Samuel 12:24 is a good place to start)? I strongly urge you to go and do so. Perhaps you should also read about the very wealthy young man who asked Jesus what he could do to inherit the Kingdom of God (Mark 10:16-18). By the time Jesus finished dealing with his question, he became very sad and downcast because he was very wealthy. Basically, Jesus Christ told him to sell all he has, give to the poor and needy and then come and follow Jesus.

Our several "servants of God" of today would seize such an opportunity and testify to the whole world how God Blessed them with that type of young man (could be a woman) because they "sowed a seed" for prosperity. Beloved, be wise. Open your eyes, ears and mind to the things of the Spirit. The things that we see are so very temporal; it is those things that we do not see that are eternal (2 Corinthians 4:18). Seek the Lord whilst He may be found; for a time is coming and is very close now as surely as Jesus Christ Lives forevermore, when it will be too late to seek after Him. Then Judgement will be our lot.

Let the reader know that the reality of the coming of our Lord Jesus Christ cannot be overemphasised. He is coming soon (Revelation 3:11; 22:7,12,20). Why make hay when the sun is no longer shining? It is as good as making hay when the rains are pouring. Now, today, is the time/day for your redemption and salvation. The ultimate sacrifice (Jesus Christ Crucified as evidenced in the Holy Scriptures – John 19) has been made and the price paid in full for you and for me to come to fulfil the destiny of man in Jesus Christ. All who want to be saved from the coming destruction should act now. Come to Jesus and not delay.

Whether we like it or not, those who believe and obey the trumpet call to come to Jesus Christ are to God the aroma of Christ (2 Corinthians 2:15-16) among those who are being saved and those who are perishing. To the former, we are as a sweet aroma and to the latter a horrible stench. Still, this world has nothing to offer us that can last. Your wealth will not last. Your body will not last either. All the make-up in the world serves only to assuage your fleshly desires and will never satisfy you.

All the jewellery in the world will perish likewise. The finest oils, perfumery, clothing, houses, jets, cars and most gorgeous hair dos and all these worldly things (James 4:4) that we so much crave to our shame will not stand the test of time. Beauty is fleeting and lust for power, wealth, etc. are a sham, very temporal, leading only to death. There is one way that seems right to a man, in the end it leads to death (Proverbs 16:12).

Wake up from your slumbered spiritual state. All the tobacco and drugs in the world will never fill up that vacuum in your soul. All the charitable giving and works will not do. You can think you are a good person and hide behind your several masks and finger(s) but when the Light Shines upon you is when the Truth will be Revealed and this will surely happen.

You say you are good and in fact you who claim to be Godly and continue to act wickedly and when it is within your power to help even a servant of God, you turn the other side or make it even more difficult. That is when you remember all the codes of practice that you never kept to when doing favours for your family and friends, even when they did not need the help.

The Bible says not to forget to entertain strangers (Hebrews 13:12). You may just be entertaining our Lord Jesus Christ himself without knowing so. He after all, said, whatsoever you do unto one of my brothers, that you do unto me (Matthew 25:31-46).

God is watching our every move (Romans 8:27; 1 Corinthians 2:10; 1 Chronicles 28:9; Revelation 2:23). We have looked at the need for wisdom that is Godly to guide and help us run our race earlier. Whatever we do here on earth leads only to reward according to what we have sown, the race we have run and how we have competed in running our race.

How are you running yours. You may not answer now but you must some day when He shall ask of you. Then though, it will be too late. Now is when you can test and re-test and check yourself to see that you are in the Faith (2 Corinthians 13:4-6) or to come into the Faith.

This world is not our home (Ephesians 2:19; Philippians 3:20), why do you then make it yours and as if life will never end for you on earth. In fact, we shall all die some day and whither to? The Bible tells us to forsake the world. It is not profitable to love the world at the expense of the loss of our souls unto eternal damnation. What is it about this world that causes us to opt for this world and its lusts and not for what is profitable unto eternity, even Eternal Life?

Sin and the attending laxities and sweetness thereof are the baits that this world offers us to catch us out and bend us into the will of the devil. We love the world so much because we love to be like the other people we see and perceive to be very successful and we begin to model our thoughts words and deeds after such without knowing their history and where they will end up.

We train up our children with the potential we gained in our own parents training us – to succeed in life mostly, rather than to succeed in Jesus Christ in living a life pleasing unto God (Ecclesiastes 2:26, 7:26; Romans 8:8; 1 Thessalonians 4:1-11). The children do the same with their children and the trend goes on.

The curse perpetuates as a result of our folly from one generation to the next (Deuteronomy 5:8-10). We strive after all sorts of idols to enhance our cultivation of happiness and success. We are ready to lie, cheat, kill, aid murder, bear false witness, set others up for evil reasons and do anything to protect our territory. Often our territory is built on false foundations and terrains that we whitewash and make to look ever so nice and good.

We however remain shattered within and unfulfilled. When we are in this state, we have a dire need to wear masks to hide what is inside so that others do not see anything other than what we show them. We live daily, but a lie. In this mode, our drive is increasingly for world acclaim, success and commendations. We envy others, we are arrogant, rude, unkind, wicked and perverse.

We chase after and revel in sexual immorality and or perversions, witchcraft, wizardry, sorcery, occult, freemasonry, etc.; we crave for knowledge (but not of God in Jesus Christ), we gamble, engage in drugs, we want for more intake of alcohol, drugs, smoke (even drugs and dangerous intoxicating herbs and substances). All these are temporary highs and lows depending on individual balance and levels of participation and or usage.

We are driven very gradually, but surely away from God. We love the music, dance and cultures depicting the way of the world and its idols to the tempter's delight (i.e. satan). Can we please God this way? The Bible says in Romans 8:8 that those who revel in the sinful nature cannot please God. Rather than hate the world and love the Lord and seek to please Him, we love and revel in the world against the Word of God in James 4:4 that encourages us not to love the world otherwise we are enemies of God.

Yet, the Word of God is so very close to us (Deuteronomy 30:14; Romans 10:8-11), able to reunite us with the God who truly loves us so much as to Enable His Son to come (John 3:16) to us for the purposes of offering us salvation in believing in His Name and His Sacrifice, believing in Him. All God requires of us is simply to believe and this we find so hard? We allow satan to rule our lives.

Satan deceives us as he wanted to do to Jesus Christ at the end of forty days and forty nights of fasting. He tested Jesus Christ three times, especially with the offer of the whole world (his domain supposedly) as a package of treasures. Jesus Christ stood firm as an example for us to follow through with the Word of God and His Promises. Jesus Christ fought satan off with the Weapons of Righteousness in God's Word (Matthew 4:1-11). Do note that satan used the Word of God even in the tempting of Jesus. So do not think that you can be wise like satan and be self secure or self sufficient to deal with satan at all.

Jesus Christ strongly urged us to seek first the Kingdom of God and His Righteousness and all things shall be added unto us (Matthew 6:23). Our needs shall be taken care of when we give up our worldly life to follow Jesus Christ, entering into His Righteousness.

Do note here that Jesus Christ never begged or sought to please anyone into following Him at all. We see today's so-called servants of God pleading and practically on their knees begging the world to come to Jesus. It is no wonder that there is such moral laxity, decadence and very little or no fear of God in a vast majority of peoples today.

We have presented the Word of God as so weak to save and or deliver. God Will yet Glorify Himself and Prove His Worthiness to be feared. Therefore, we need not seek after worldly gains and or treasures as a matter of priority at all. After all, wherever your treasure is, there your heart will be also (Matthew 6:19-22). These are the things that keep us far from God and vice-versa. Rather, we ought to seek for the Kingdom of God to be established in our hearts and souls and minds. What a difference Jesus Christ makes in our lives when we focus and strive to work hard (not for what cannot last, but for what is eternal).

When we walk with the Lord in the Light of His Love what a Glory He Sheds on our way; as we do His good Will, Jesus Christ will continue to abide with us still, as with all who choose to trust and obey Him. Only then can we truly consider such Love that Jesus Christ Showed to us in offering Himself on the cross at Calvary just for our salvation. What a glorious example and life we have been privileged to come to know in and through Jesus Christ our Lord.

Who else can save us from this world of sin? What can wash us white as snow and wash away our sins and Bless us with a new life? Nothing else but the Blood of Jesus can make us clean and whole again. Who have we in Heaven besides Him? No one. We must honour Him and Him alone; desire only Him forevermore. Our hearts and strengths may fail sometimes yes; but God is our Strength even in Jesus Christ. Amen. For when we are weak, we are strong; and when we are poor, we are rich. In our weaknesses, the Power of our Lord Jesus Christ is made perfect (2 Corinthians 12:9).

The Kingdom of God...

Beloved, there is a structure to the Kingdom of God; and there is a Standard to Guide its functioning. This is why we have the Holy Bible as a veritable manual for learning about God and His Word. It is in Him that we find ourselves eventually, when we diligently put His Word to practice. In God through Jesus Christ we see Light (Psalm 36:9; Isaiah 9:2; Exodus 10:22-24; 2 Corinthians 4:4) and our darkness will surely disintegrate as we become increasingly filled with Light.

I will do my best with the Help of Almighty God in Christ Jesus to effectively highlight a means of communicating to you my reader, the profitability of opening our hearts to receive the Kingdom of God into our lives. There is no richer treasure. I have read the many testimonies of those men and women of the Faith who have gone before us; and some still here with us. I have studied over and over the Holy Scriptures and I can confirm that there is no richer Treasure we can have in life and after this life as we know it. I speak of my own experience and this confirmed by the testimonies of so many others.

God is King and Jesus Christ His Son is affirmed right through the Holy Scriptures as equal with God (Philippians 2:5-7) in Royal Majesty as attested to in the Book of John, Chapter 1. For it is written that God is One with Jesus Christ all through the Bible.

From the beginning of time, the Word was with God and is God. Jesus Christ is confirmed as God. This is a mystery of our Faith and is not to be received with the human understanding, senses and sensibilities, but rather with and by faith. The Holy Bible makes it abundantly clear that they that believe (the just) must live by faith

(Romans 1:17; 4:14) and not lean upon their own understanding (Proverbs 3:5).

Feelings (sensual perceptions etc.) are the bane of and upon which human judgements are made. We know that feelings are very unreliable in essence, through experience. Hence, the need for an emphasis on objectivity in today's largely science-driven world and we play down any subjective evidence in terms of reality. Feelings we mostly agree tend to follow after and reflect the heart. What does the Word of God have to say about the human heart? It is deceitful and desperately wicked (Jeremiah 17:9).

Be attentive to receive what God has to say about the human heart. Very interestingly, the Holy Word of God declares that the heart of mankind is deceptive and desperately wicked. A big scream is suppressed in my throat even now just to comprehend the extent and depth of this revealed wisdom. Who can know the heart of man? So can I really rely on my feelings in any situation? Yet, there are many teachers out there who only follow after mere instincts like animals. Yet, they claim that they have the Holy Spirit.

Can you trust your own feelings/instincts or those who rely on theirs and manipulate yours with skilful words rooted in human knowledge and understanding? If I cannot rely nor lean upon my own understanding, feelings, instincts, even heart, which by nature is inclined unto evil and wickedness, then I need help. In a world where the order of the day is based on and driven by people who are driven by such a condemned human resource, where do I stand the chance? I am potentially finished in my flesh.

Thanks be unto our Lord Jesus Christ however, for He always causes us to triumph, providing a way out for us (always) to escape out of our many troubles and afflictions (1 Corinthians 10:13). We have (on the Authority of the Holy Bible) a sure Word of God that where all else fails (John 16:33; 1 John 4:4; 1 John 5;5), we can, as a matter of Righteousness, Truth, Justice and Wisdom from God, rely upon Jesus Christ. We are strongly urged and encouraged to put our whole and full trust upon and lean on Him.

In His Royal Majesty, Jesus Christ offers us great and profitable Counsel regarding the Kingdom of God (Heaven) and how we can prepare for and enter therein. Only through Jesus Christ can we enter into the Kingdom of God. No one can come to God except through the Son of God, Jesus Christ, unblemished, the Lamb of God. Amen (John 14:6).

This is a source of concern for a substantial majority on earth for they lean upon their own senses and understanding. The very account of the existence of Jesus Christ is incomprehensible for many. Yet, there is historical evidence beyond all doubts that a Supreme Sacrifice was paid for us to have this access to God through the crucifixion of Jesus Christ on the cross for the salvation of humanity. This is for those who believe though.

All who do not believe stand condemned already (John 3:16-18), regardless of the Supreme Love that Offered Him who had no sin as a sacrifice; made to carry all our sinfulness and to atone for our sinful nature and reconcile us back to God.

It is for this reason that the Name of Jesus Christ has become so far entrenched in humanity, waxing stronger, even after over two thousand years of efforts to discredit this Wonderful Story. This great story given unto us has been vehemently discredited in order to ensure that the Name of Jesus Christ is not spread as God Almighty, made manifest unto humanity for the salvation of the lost souls of those who dare to receive and believe Him.

There is only one way to God; all others are futile and any impostors a waste of time and effort. Why would God choose to invest in us only for us to be reconciled back to Him through One Way? He alone Knows and who is man to question Him? For sure though, no other man ever lived on earth declaring to be ONE with God and that He is the Way, Truth and Life. Jesus Christ is His name and He is the Lord God Almighty. Amen.

Entry Through the Gate...

Jesus Christ declared with Power that He is the Gateway to the Father. All are thieves who attempt to (or) enter through any other route(s). Jesus Christ declared with Power that He is the Good Shepherd (John 10:1-21).

If we attend for a party or function to which we have been invited; and we get to the gate that leads into the premises where the function is taking place, that is our entry point. Our journey to that point is our entry route. Often in the world we live in today, such a gate is manned either by a human or by machine (electronically). Whichever way, we need certified access (human security personnel and or an electronic pass) for entry.

With the Kingdom of God, the only access we need and must have is Jesus Christ, who is, was and forever shall be. Amen. Right through the Holy Scriptures, it is very evident that Jesus Christ has been Revealed from the very beginning. So much so that a very old man (Simeon) declared that the God of Israel should now dismiss His servant in peace as his eyes beheld the Salvation of Israel (at the birth of Jesus Christ (Luke 2:25-38) – on the eighth day). The Bible clearly says Jesus is both author and finisher of our faith (Hebrews 12:2).

Jesus Christ has been present from the beginning, is now and will be at the end (Revelations 1:8). Amen. For all to whom it is Granted to come to Jesus Christ, this testimony is vital for a witness to the reality of Jesus Christ.

No one can come to the Lord except the Lord Himself Draws one by Himself (John 6:44). However, Jesus Christ forces no one to come to Him at all; nor does He beg anyone to come to Him. When

Jesus called unto Himself all that are heavy laden (Matthew 11:28), He never begged. Jesus Christ is Revealed unto His own through the testimony of those whom He has Sent (Romans 10:14-16) to preach His Message and make disciples of people.

By the Special Grace of God, those who hear the Message, by faith, are drawn to God through hearing (Romans 10:16-18) the Message and are Granted to believe. This is not for all and sundry at all as it is presented today, which is very false. Not everyone can or will believe. However, I urge you to stand yourself in good stead to believe.

Hence, Jesus Christ declared that His sheep hear His Voice and come to Him (John 10:1-21, 26-28). I am a witness, as many others (too) to this Truth as Revealed in the Holy Scripture. Only through Jesus Christ and the attending Grace of His Holy Spirit is it made possible for any one at all to believe. Faith is Given. Granted. Faith is a Gift from God (1 Corinthians 12:9). Without faith no one can please the Lord and without holiness, no one will see the Lord (Hebrews 11:6; Hebrews 12:14). All human activity and perceived goodness without faith is futile (Romans 9:32, 14:23). To please God you must believe.

Of Faith...

To believe in God and in His Son, Jesus Christ is paramount to the Christian Faith. Faith in this Great God, who Sent His Son (One and Only) to die for us, is what Christianity is based on. Again, there is no way anyone can please God without this faith (Hebrews 11:5-7). Therefore to get anywhere at all on this journey, in this race, you must believe that God is real and that Jesus Christ is His Son. You must believe the Sacrifice of Jesus Christ on the Cross and His Resurrection on the third day; that the whole Jesus Christ story is REAL, Truthful and for eternity.

The Holy Bible describes faith in the way that it must be understood in the spiritual sense for the purposes of coming to know and to follow God through Jesus Christ. The Bible says that faith is being sure of what you hope for and certain of what you have not seen (Hebrews 11:1).

Faith therefore is not seeing is believing (the human senses and sensibility view of reality). I will believe when I see etc. is the worldly viewpoint. That is totally opposite to faith in Jesus Christ (God). In faith, you live in trust and hope for the certainty that the object of your hope will come to pass. Nobody hopes for what they have already received (Romans 8:24). So, faith is about what you have not yet received, but sure to get.

The faithful just trust that what they hope for will surely manifest without failing in due season. This applies in a very "live" (real) way. This is to say that the faith under our discourse is alive and does not die. This faith is a living faith in a living God and exists on an infinite basis, in a continuum. Faith reflects past, present and future.

Faith reflects the past in that although (for example) I was not there to witness this happening, I believe. There is a witness within me in my spirit that knows for sure that the object of my faith is certainly, assuredly true, so, I believe. Faith relates to the present in that (likewise) although I am here now, I need no proof to believe. I just believe. In relation to the future, faith says likewise (as above) that, I will believe; no matter what, regardless of proof/evidence, my believing will neither shake nor change.

The way of man is to see and believe as a result of having seen. To experience with the senses and thus know, is to believe, for the natural, sinful nature. However, with God, only faith will do.

God is pleased when He Knows that you do trust Him in everyway and God Will become very real for you, if you will dare to believe and show Him in your living, that, you actually do trust Him fully.

Many say that they do not believe in the existence of God and yet hate and or despise those who do believe for believing. I say there is an element of jealousy here; and perhaps envy, leading on from a frustration in not believing since the mindset is programmed not to believe without evidence. So the unbeliever wonders why, how come "they" believe and "I" am unable to understand or believe.

There is an underlying knowledge that all these people who believe in God cannot all be liars and as such must have something very special, that the non-believer does not have. This manifests in the negative behaviour and attitude described above. This anger is often of a covert nature, due to not having this "special" knowing of God's reality (faith in God).

This hatred is rooted in a hidden knowledge of and reflection in the fact that, there is probably a God and that He is probably very real for all these others to believe in Him (albeit ridiculous to the one who has not yet had the revelation). This reality is so sorely missed therefore by the one who does not believe; and the prideful, arrogant nature takes over. This manifests in the negative behaviour towards the believers.

A lot can be written around the issue of faith, but my current message is to highlight the subject in a way that will serve both to assure and challenge the reader regardless of their faith in God (Jesus). The importance of faith cannot be overemphasised; for, to please God, is the object of the believer's journey; in order to reach the goal. I am not suggesting that it is very easy to want to believe.

This is not however sufficient for the purpose of living a life of holiness at all. Yet, Jesus Christ has been our Help in encouraging us to have faith. Even His wisdom to us that, if we have faith as small as a mustard seed, we shall experience wonders – even saying to this mountain to be removed and cast into the seas and it will obey us.

I am strongly urging and encouraging you my reader to dig deeper. If you have/had a concept of faith, whether you practice it or not, begin to put it to practice. If you have never had this concept you now have so much to chew on and meditate upon, so as to begin to put this new learning into practice.

One thing is certain. This writer has had this concept for a long many years; and will readily witness and testify to the reality of God in Christ Jesus. Likewise, in the effective operation of faith that works through love, to be evident in the life of anyone who will follow the teachings of Jesus Christ and make Him Lord over all in one's life.

To Believe...

Again let me reiterate that, to have faith is to believe; and this is the manifestation of a heart that is rooted in Love for God in Jesus Christ. To believe is to respond to the Message of the Gospel of Jesus Christ in a practical, positive, life changing way. The Message of Jesus Christ is rooted in the beginning as stated in the first Book of John (John 1:1-5). John wrote as the Holy Spirit Inspired him; that, Jesus Christ is, from the very beginning, the Word of God. He wrote that Jesus Christ is God.

This is a veritable bone of contention amongst many, as human beings are predisposed to lean upon their own understanding. To believe, is to believe in the existence of God; and to believe in His Son Jesus Christ; and to believe in God's Power and Ability to Do all things. This is to know that nothing is impossible for God regardless of how impossible things may be for mankind (Luke 1:37, 18:27).

To believe is to be so drawn to God as to love Him deeply beyond all else including life itself and all it has to offer in a manner of living. To believe is to know beyond any human reasoning that God Sent His Word (Jesus Christ) according to the Holy Scriptures prophesied from of old (Galatians 4:3-5; Isaiah 9:5-7; Hosea 11: 1-3; 1 John 4:8-11). To believe the fact that the story of Jesus Christ's prophetic manifestation on earth, His sacrifice, death, ascension and promise of a second coming is actually true.

This truth, having been revealed through a most Supernatural Conception of the Holy Spirit (Luke 1:25-32; 2:1-3) by a virgin (Mary), who had been pledged to marry Joseph, but came to be with child (Jesus Christ – Isaiah 7:13-15; Matthew 1:22-24) through no human knowledge of (being intimate with) a man.

Jesus Christ was born into the world naturally, of woman; without the woman having known a man through sexual intimacy via intercourse. To believe this; and also that this birth took place in a manger (Luke 2:6-17), under very humble circumstances (in a sheep's pen more or less) is to believe.

To believe the account of the Gospels as in the Holy Scriptures that this Jesus Christ laid down His life for the salvation of mankind as predestined by God, is, to believe. There is so much more to believing. Not only did Jesus Christ die, He had a prophetic (pre-destined) purpose in laying down His life.

It was also predestined that, to save humanity from eternal damnation, Jesus Christ became as a human sacrifice, even as Abraham was willing to sacrifice Isaac. Abraham had also consented to this willingly, believing his God and Father. For this reason was Abraham justified and Blessed to be the father of faith. His believing God earned Him such a Divine grace, for God to count his believing, his faith, unto him, as righteousness (Romans 4:3; Galatians 3:6; James 2:23).

Jesus Christ is God in human flesh (John 1:1-3) who came to His own creation and died to save them. So much so that we are able to recognise God's Spirit in humanity in that any spirit that fails to acknowledge that Jesus Christ, our Lord and God, came to humanity in the flesh is not from God (1 John 4:1-3). Greater Love has no man than this – for a man to lay down His life for His friends – the greatest love of all. It took Jesus Christ Himself to pay the ultimate price, a ransom for our sinfulness as humans.

As predestined, after three days, Jesus Christ Rose again from the dead (Mark 8:30-32; 9:30-32; Matthew 27:62-64) and Revealed Himself to many of His disciples (Luke 20:17-29) before ascending up into the Heavens in the presence of witnesses (Luke 24:48-53). Anyone who believes will be very much drawn to this Greatest

Story (Love) of all time; and in being so drawn, will learn of the Sacrifice par Excellence, Jesus Christ. Jesus Christ Himself said that the proof of anyone's love for Him (hence, faith in Him) is to obey His Commandments (John 14:15; 1 John 5:2-3) and do the Will of the Father.

I am amazed always that human beings cannot fathom the depths of the love of God for us. Yet, I should not be. This brain that we have; and the capacity to think and make choices, is very deceptive. Of course, the brain works directly with the heart; considering what God said about the heart (Jeremiah 17:9), no wonder. We go around the world as if we have answers to all problems. Alas, it is all a farce. Only God can save us. Only Jesus Christ can save. Even when disasters hit us, we cry for God.

Somehow, lying dormant in most humans is the predisposition to believe. How so very awesome.

To be Born Again...

Anyone who believes must be born again of the Spirit and of water. This is to be born again according to the Testimony of Jesus Christ in John Chapter 3. The testimony was pre-empted by John the Baptist, who although called people (preached to them) onto repentance, baptised them in water.

John the Baptist however warned them all of the coming of Jesus Christ, who was already in their midst and would baptise them with the Holy Spirit and with fire (Luke 3:16; Matthew 3:11). This testimony is attested to as sure and even repeated in the testimony of John the disciple, Chapter 1.

As Promised by Jesus Christ, His Holy Spirit was indeed Sent and manifested on the Day of Pentecost (Acts 2). The Holy Spirit came down as a ball of fire, separated and rested as tongues of fire, on each of the one hundred and twenty disciples waiting in the Upper Room, as Instructed by Jesus Christ. Through the manifestation of the Holy Spirit and the resulting impact, each of the disciples spoke in different tongues and all who were witnessing this heard them, each in his own language.

Being born again includes to repent of one's sinful past and receive forgiveness of sins in Jesus' Name; then, to pledge one's conscience (anew) to the Lord Jesus Christ and prove that pledge with deeds commensurate with repentance (Acts 26:20). This is the promise to forsake the old sinful self and to trust in Jesus Christ's Holy Name for leadership through the Holy Spirit. The believer must remember that as many as are led by the Holy Spirit are the sons of the Living God (Romans 8:13-15).

To be born again is to submit to being filled with the Holy Spirit and yielding to the Holy Spirit's Leading and Direction. Only by fully submitting to the Holy Spirit can the mind of the believer be renewed. Prior to believing, the mind is heavily corrupted with the world. But on accepting Jesus Christ as Lord and Saviour and accepting His Message regarding the Kingdom of God, the believer enters into a covenant of love (Daniel 9:4; Ezekiel 16:8; 2 Chronicles 16:14; Nehemiah 1:5) and attending transformation increasingly into the likeness of the Perfect One, Jesus Christ, Holy God. Amen.

In becoming born again and believing, one covenants with Jesus Christ no longer to serve satan, be enslaved to or be bonded with the world and its ways, no longer to be unequally yoked with unbelievers (2 Corinthians 6:14). Rather, the covenant is to be yoked with the yoke of Jesus Christ (the Word of God), which is easy, the burden of whom is light (Matthew 11:28-30).

The believer, learning to wait upon the Holy Spirit for Direction, must worship God in Christ Jesus in spirit and in truth (John 4:22-24). To believe and be born again is to flee from and forsake all forms of idolatry and love for the world and its evil wicked desires (2 Timothy 2:22), based upon diverse lusts of the flesh and senses. To believe is to pray ceaselessly (1 Thessalonians 5:16-18), be of good cheer, be of Godly disposition in thoughts, words and deeds as befits a follower of Jesus Christ.

A Price to Pay...

Believe me beloved; when I say that there is a price to pay, even for love. You may not wish to hear or read about this. This will however not change the Truth. Many preach today that Jesus Christ already paid the price. Yes, but we who believe must fellowship with His Sufferings (Philippians 3:9-11; 1 Peter 4:11-14; Romans 8:16-18; 2 Corinthians 1:4-6).

This is made very clear in the Word of God and many ignore this to their own shame and ultimate destruction. Jesus Christ Himself paid the Ultimate Price for the propitiation of our sins. God Gave Jesus Christ as a ransom, a price to pay; and that was paid for my/our redemption.

What this means in effect is that God Gave of Himself. God actually Gave Himself for us. In the parable of the tenants, Jesus spoke in the New Testament about a landowner who leased out his land for others to farm. They in turn were to give back to him a percentage of their harvest, annually. The leaseholders defaulted (Matthew 21:33-41).

The landowner sent his son in the hope that the leaseholders would see him in his son and honour him (having killed the first couple of trusted aides sent), to pay their dues. No, they killed him instead. In so doing they automatically incurred the wrath of the landowner, regardless of his graciousness and or mercy to the leaseholders. They in turn will pay a price. For all things good or bad there is a price to pay.

When a father disciplines his son (Hebrews 12), he is paying a price, even to procure a future for that child. The Bible tells us in the Book of Proverbs that to spare the rod is to spoil the child (Proverbs

13:24; 23:12-14). I want my reader to ponder and understand deeply; and know, beyond any doubts whatsoever, that God has put in place structures and laws to order the whole universe and cosmic environment. This includes mankind who live on earth, in living on and taking control of managing (subduing) the earth (Genesis 1:28).

To emphasise again the point that a price has to be paid – it is written in the Word of God Authoritatively that we were bought (all who believe) with/at a price (1 Corinthians 6:19-20). Therefore, to dare to believe is to accept this fact of having been purchased at a price and are therefore enslaved unto Christ Jesus (1 Corinthians 7:22; Ephesians 6:4-7) through the bond of wilful obedience.

Obedience to the Master, thus being in turn, our price for whatever freedom He has Procured for us as a result. Hence, we have power to tread over lions, snakes and scorpions etc. (Luke 7:18-20). We are overcomers (1 John 2:12-15; 1 John 5:3-6; Revelations 12:11) through Jesus Christ and can do all things through Jesus Christ who gives us Strength (Philippians 4:13). Amen.

In reading these words, even for the writer, they come alive. For as the Word is indeed of God, the Word Lives. The letter kills, but the Spirit gives life (2 Corinthians 3:6; John 6:63). The Word is active because it has life in it (Hebrews 4:12).

Because of the life in the Word, the Word Lives; hence, it is called the Living Word. These words must live within the person who truly believes. Jesus said, if you abide in Me and allow my Words to abide in you, then you will ask for what you desire and I will Answer (John 15:4-8). This Word will be written on the hearts of the true believers (Hebrews 8:10, 10:16; Proverbs 3:3, 7:3; Romans 2:14-16). A price must be paid for the Word to flow, just like the Blood of Jesus Christ which flowed was the price paid for our salvation, for those who believe.

For the righteous, any of their blood that is shed for the sake of Jesus Christ is holy and will never die. Their blood lives forever, just as Abel's blood still speaks today (Hebrews 11:4), having been shed for no just cause, except for righteousness' sake (given that Cain killed him for reasons of envy/jealousy).

Abel's sacrifice was accepted by God, whilst Cain's was rejected; hence, his murder by his brother, Cain (Genesis 4:8). The Blood of Jesus Christ washes white as snow (Psalm 51:7; Isaiah 1:18). A case of the dilemma of humanity is that when asked, most people will say they want to go to heaven, but none of them want to die. Not wanting to die is not wanting to pay the price.

Yes, Jesus Christ paid the Ultimate Price, however, if we do not fellowship with His sufferings we have no part in Him really. To love Jesus Christ involves to be able and willing and ready to suffer anything in His Name even unto death. One has to carry one's cross, deny oneself and follow Him (Luke 9:23-27).

This is never an easy experience. Only the Holy Spirit makes it easier for us to bear living a holy life for and in Christ Jesus on a day to day basis. Jesus said He will never leave nor forsake us (Hebrews 13:5).

Jesus Christ Himself is the Holy Spirit (John 14:17-19; John 16:7, 12-16) who walks and talks with us and will lead us into all truth and all righteousness, if we truly are His sons (as many as are led by the Holy Spirit). So, I declare to you with love dear reader that there is pain in love and there is not true love without pain and discipline (Hebrews 12). There is a price to pay.

Someone may say to me what kind of nonsense am I going on about. However, a proverb says that half a word is enough for the wise. When we look up to Jesus Christ and want to live for Him, we then study His own example as we have the privilege and opportunity to do so. This generation is very privileged in this way.

In all of life we live and struggle with living whilst sojourning on this earth. What the Holy Scriptures do for us in the Name of the Merciful God is to Enable us to live with some guidance from God. When we obey, it means we have to give up on what most of the world consider so very important. What marks us out as believers, is our ability to prove the life of Christ is more fulfilling, in not indulging in the desires of our flesh, which is what the world revel in. This is the crux of the true Christian life.

Love Hurts...

I have declared in the Name of our Father through Jesus Christ and from His own example that love hurts. How much God must hurt seeing the way we live on earth with so much deceit, wickedness and sin. God was so disappointed that He destroyed His creation in the days of Noah (Genesis 7:13,23). Sodom and Gomorrah was likewise destroyed (Genesis 19:12-13, 23-26).

God is Love and Love is God. Love hurts and God hurts. God is not pleased that humanity should suffer. But God has Given us that choice to choose what is good and Godly (Deuteronomy 30:10; 2 Kings 18:32).

Before you read on please pause for a moment and let us explore meditatively the matter of this painful loving that is holy. Let us consider that God is Love and God is Holy. Even as God is Loving and Kind and Generous and all, God is an all consuming Fire (Deuteronomy 4:24; Hebrews 12:29) and is an Awesome God (Exodus 15:11; Deuteronomy 7:21; Psalm 89:7).

Let us consider that Jesus Christ is the Word of God and the Word of God is considered as sharper than any double-edged sword (Hebrews 4:12). Let us not think for a moment that this was not God's Plan, because it has been from the beginning. This is the only way it will work for any believer to live a holy life.

Jesus Christ had to go through it same way. This Jesus Christ is from of old. He is the Ancient Of Days. The Holy One. The Way to Him is the same; the Ancient Path (Jeremiah 6:15-17). The One and only Way, with no short cuts. To avoid this Way is to miss the Way completely.

Even as the rough, uncut diamonds must go through a process of purification to come out glittering as they do, so it is with the followers of the Way and so it must be. We must accept that it is not an easy road we are travelling to heaven and that there will be pain, thorns etc. on the way. No one can quantify or prepare for how much of the pains we shall encounter.

This is where the instruction we have from Jesus Christ that the righteous must live by faith (Habakkuk 2:4; Romans 1:17; Galatians 3:11; Hebrews 10:38) comes in very handy. When we accept this fact then we can begin to learn to live a holy life. There is no one who wants to live a Godly life in Christ Jesus for instance, who will not be persecuted (2 Timothy 3:12). So, beloved get ready. However, it is well worth every pain (James 1:2-8).

For this very reason, many cannot and will not live a holy life for they love the pleasures of life more than God. They love the world more than Jesus Christ and it is not very difficult to know them. The Bible warns against such people and their teaching spreads very fast (2 Peter 2). They are popular with everybody and always want to be acclaimed by men. They make their own way in life and pretend to be servants of God. They confess Jesus Christ as Lord God and all but their hearts are far removed from Jesus Christ (Matthew 15:8-10).

This wicked world offers too much in terms of idolatry. Idolatry is good looking, smells excellently to our senses; mostly invoking in us, a sensuality that arouses unholiness in us. Emotionally and spiritually, the ways of the world invokes lots of sensuality and freedom especially in a sexual way. Hence, the superior Word of God urging us to flee from sexual immorality (1 Corinthians 6:17-19).

Check out any practices of idolatry and there is so much sex involved that it becomes so unreal. For this reason many abstain from sex because they are so fed up with the severity of perversion involved. This is not to say that such people are Godly. They are simply damaged and suffering a satanic backlash. They soon return to their vomit anyway.

There is an alarming consistency in the evil practices within idolaters' gatherings. They practice their faith in a very strict and sacrificial way. They call their gatherings all sorts of names and give each other names and engage in the most unthinkable levels of decadence. They very rigidly worship their idols and show no shame at all except to hide from fellow human beings and escape the laws of the land. They usually have contacts in very high places who help to hide their evil. The Bible urges us to expose them (Ephesians 5:11-13).

As for us so-called believers, we abuse the word (love) so freely without even truly ever really understanding the meaning and depth of life potential in the word love. Love can only cover a multitude of sins because of its very nature. Love cannot be without discipline. Discipline, like discipleship, is a very painful process, even like a child being born in child bearing.

A child is not just born as a matter of eating and drinking and toileting. No. The male and female meet and share (contribute) seed and egg respectively through a process of intercourse. The unit thus formed is embedded in the woman's members and only God knows the secret of how the baby is actually made real; and life begets life within the woman's body.

The woman carries the baby for a period of time and gives birth through a very painful process. Despite the pain, there is tremendous joy when the child is born (John 16:21). It is so ordained by God for a reason and will never be an easy process. Likewise, the process of learning to love and loving cannot be without pain.

When a child is truly loved, given love and also well cared for, the child is carefully trained with the rod by the parents. Such a child, even in receiving the rod, learns to deal with pain, both physically and spiritually, in the journey of life. Otherwise, a child cannot ever cope in this world.

God did not encourage pain as a means of punishing us and making our lives a misery. No. God intended for us to be trained and come out strong to deal with life's diverse issues. God is not a horrible God. God wants us to be strong.

This is why Jesus Christ encourages us to take His yoke upon us and cast off the yoke of satan (Matthew 11:28-30). The reason being that the yoke of Jesus Christ is easy and His burden is light. We are instructed in God's Word not to be unequally yoked with unbelievers (2 Corinthians 6:14-15).

Again, in learning to bow to the parents, the child begins to learn the need to respect and bow to the teachers at school. In so doing, this child learns to bear pain. For pain is not just when punished with the rod. Pain comes with controlling the individual ego and keeping it in check. That is to say you may want or feel like having something. This does not mean that you can have it.

It can be painful not to be able to have what one wants. That is a type of pain. In life, we go through some issues and will face some levels of offence from others sometimes; and sometimes others will step on our toes. We do the same too sometimes. So we must learn to give and take.

To live a Godly life in Christ Jesus we must be able to bear pain. This is referred to as longsuffering, as in love (1 Corinthians 13). This is an attribute of love. This is a dynamic process.

Understandably it is with the mindset of a child (pure and without evil judgements based upon misguided thoughts nurtured in unholy anger and hatred) that one can cope with pain in love. Jesus said we must come as little children (Mark 10:13-15). Love is something that few were/are trained to know, let alone put to practice. Hence, many cannot handle love and run when love comes. Someone said be careful what you ask for; otherwise, you might just get it. Are you ready for love? Willing to sacrifice? Well then, come along with me.

Love is a Sacrifice...

Let me go on to say that love is a living process of sacrificial giving and receiving. Giving and receiving here is not just talking about taking that which is good and nice; and not wanting anything otherwise. Shall we take what is good from the Lord and not want a part of suffering in His Name (Job 2:10)?

Love must give and take in a balanced dynamic way, so dynamic as to mature over time increasingly. It is this mastering and maturing of this process in a believer that determines whether or not they are ready for meat or still need milk (Hebrews 5:11-14).

Human knowledge and understanding always runs contrary to this sacrificial love because satan is very determined to ensure that as many people as possible be bound.

True freedom is to learn the wisdom of love. Jesus Christ is the Wisdom of God. The Wisdom of God is Love. The Bible says that the sacrifices of God are as a broken spirit and a contrite heart, which God Will never ignore, when reliant upon Him (Psalm 51:17).

This is why it is that Jesus Christ is close to such as are broken and of contrite hearts. Jesus Christ is very close to the hurting, the damaged, the widows, orphans, those in prisons etc.

Jesus Christ came to set the captives free (Luke 4:17-19). Amongst other things like giving sight to the blind, Jesus Christ is the author and finisher of our faith.

Hence, Jesus Christ is our Supreme example of sacrificial love. When we meditate on the sacrifice of Jesus Christ, one finds that there is tremendous power with great potential in sacrificial love.

This is why Jesus Christ told us that before anything can grow, first, like a grain of wheat in the soil, it has to die (1 Corinthians 15:36). Afterwards, a great harvest is reaped from what seemed absolutely dead.

This is a great lesson in life. It is for this reason that Jesus Christ gave His life, knowing that a great harvest will follow.

You must be ready to sacrifice for and in love. No matter the relationship. Especially with Jesus Christ of course; but this is applicable in marriage, friendship (true friendship is rare though), working relations etc.

Remember that there is nothing impossible for God; if you are willing to try, God Will take you all the way. Can you forgive? Can you be devoted to Jesus Christ? If you can, nothing will be impossible for you, if you will follow His Ways.

Jesus Christ, Lamb of God...

When Abraham was requested to sacrifice his one and only son, who would have known he would simply comply, especially after promises of him going to be a great nation and all? How many of us will obey? We will argue, even be rude and shout at God and probably curse Him if that were possible. We are so bad mannered in our approach to the Holy God.

God's thoughts and ways are very much higher and very far and different than ours. This story of Abraham (Genesis 22:6-8; Hebrews 11:17-18) was symbolising the future sacrifice of Jesus Christ. It is just too similar (close) to be absolutely unconnected.

However, a major difference in the physical reality is the provision of a lamb (in the case of Abraham) for sacrifice to replace Isaac, Abraham's only son. Whereas, in the case of our Lord Jesus Christ, He Himself served as the unblemished Lamb for sacrifice. Either way, God Provided for sacrifice in both cases. God is the Great Provider (Genesis 22:14).

Note that Isaac was not only told, he was prepared, he had been trained appropriately in the fear of God, he was willing to obey his father, in obedience to God. Isaac had been taught God's Way. Please take time to think this through. He was only a young boy of under ten years.

He was willing to die, because God, His father's God, who became His God; and anything this Great God that he had been taught about Directed was and is, for a Higher purpose, worthy to be obeyed. What childlike faith. So, Isaac was willing and even helped to prepare an alter on which he himself was to be sacrificed. God is Great beyond measure. It is no wonder God honoured Abraham.

If those were days like today, Abraham would probably have spent the rest of his life in jail for child abuse and Isaac taken into care. These many warped minded people of today, believing they possess all knowledge or higher knowledge than most would say the boy was brainwashed and forced to follow daddy.

These people advocate for satan and occupy very high seats in government parastatals and corridors of power in every nation. They impact heavily and negatively on lives daily. There are many of them in our so-called churches today too; and thriving.

Children of God, I call upon you in the Name of Jesus Christ, beware. Test yourself. Be sure that you are still in the faith if you ever were. Jesus Christ our Lord too must have gone through a lot as a child of Joseph and Mary. Can you imagine the taunting (he must have endured) from "mates" and others.

He must have been called a bastard as some call Him even today. He was not rich either. He knew of being poor, being the son of a carpenter and never allowed to forget (Mark 6:2-4). He learnt the trade too. Hardly any mention is made, even today, of the fact that, Joseph had any part to play in His life. Joseph the humble, pious, righteous man, deemed fit to care for Mary.

Joseph was laden with the potential burden of "shame" and dishonour of marrying to a woman pregnant with child before marriage (an abomination at the time). But we live in a time when marriage, like fathers, is denigrated, despite God's Word (Hebrews 13:4).

It was not at all tolerated for a woman to be pregnant before marriage and Mary was under vows to be married to Joseph when this Great Miracle came upon her. God who is Love, Came upon her. What a life it must have been after Jesus Christ was born and for his brothers and sisters born after Him too. They must have heard that they had a strange child in the home (their "bastard" brother) from outside too.

It is a little wonder that although he learnt the trade of Joseph, the carpenter; being in very nature, God, Jesus Christ submitted to a very humble upbringing and discipline as other children were expected to do. Despite the forewarning, we learnt in the Holy Scriptures, that His mother and co-siblings, did not believe Him though. They thought he was mad, out of His mind, as in mentally unstable (Mark 3:20-22).

How frustrating this must have been for all. What turmoil that family must have faced from the community at large. Even as a baby, Herod wanted to kill him (Matthew 2:13-16). What anguish the mother must have faced and of course the father, in trying to find solutions to each problem that arose. How patient He had to have been to cope. How much He had to endure just to fulfil His destiny. What an example for all to follow; especially you, my reader and I, who may be going through endless impossibilities and thinking God forgot you. No, not necessarily so at all (Hebrews 13:3,5).

From this experience of Jesus Christ and various other Scriptural encouragements, dear reader, I want you to know that, with God, nothing is impossible (Luke 1:37). God can and will intervene for you; if you dare to learn from this message and fully trust in Him. God Will Move on your behalf. Put your faith in Him totally.

Let us remember that this is just a reflective glimpse into the possible family and community life of Jesus Christ, growing up. This also takes into consideration, the fact that the Lord's angel had told Joseph and Mary beforehand, about the birth of Jesus Christ.

I am saying that you who God has Called and you know it, do your utmost best to walk with Him very closely and search out for His Will daily.

God is a Good God (Psalm 100:5; 118). He Will speak to you. It may take longer than your expectations but do not give up, be patient. Do not be anxious at all, be at peace and be still (Psalm 46:10) and know that the Lord is God. God may not speak in the way that you are used to or know, but wait for Him and wait on Him. Be of good disposition towards Him and His Name. He Will speak to you and He Will answer your prayer according to His Word. Strive to please Him in all your thoughts, words and deeds. God surely speaks (Job 33:14-22).

So Jesus Christ suffered at the hands of the Pharisees, Sadducees, Scribes, Chief Priests etc., the custodians of God's Word, who should have recognised and embraced Him. The ridicules, jesting, lies, false accusations, gatherings of false evidence against Him etc., speak volumes in terms of what Jesus Christ had to go through on the way to the cross and not to say the burden of the whole cross and being nailed to it.

Jesus Christ was brutalised, spat upon, stripped, whipped, forced to wear a thorny crown and drink wine dregs etc. Right up until the plot to kill Him, the paying of thirty shekels to one of His disciples (for betraying Him), whom He chose like others. They shared bread together etc. The loneliness He must have felt in Revealing Himself and His Mission. The facts of His being abandoned when He was most in need (by His disciples) portray some of His sufferings too. Anyone who cannot and or will not partake of Hiis sufferings cannot be with Him. We cannot enjoy His Glory and Goodness and reject the fellowship of and with His sufferings.

Shall I not mention the thirty-nine lashes for an offence He did not commit, for which He was made to pay. The spitting and slapping His face took. How can I not mention the beatings, the anguish to the point of shedding blood and sweating as though sweating blood too, in the garden of Gethsemane (pre-arrest ordeal). Oh yes, He was robed in purple as a mockery of His Kingship. This was accompanied with much teasing, ridicule and abuse.

He was so worn out and yet expected to physically carry the cross He was going to be nailed onto. We carry an imaginary, politically correct, conceptualised cross and many of us cannot bear it. How much more did our Lord suffer. If only we would be sincere in following Him. Some of the costs are as in Matthew 8:18-22.

Let us imagine ourselves in His shoes for a moment. Tired, worn out and cross bearing. Of course, He collapsed under the full weight of the anguish He faced. Collapsing onto the ground will most likely have earned some more "wake-up" slapping around and nudges; reminiscent of the dubious, wicked nature of man. Thank God for Simon of Cyrene (Matthew 15:21), forcefully taken and made to relieve Jesus Christ of the physical burden bearing of the Cross. Simon would probably not have known the full extent of the Privilege that came His way on that Day.

A clearly despised man, passing by on his way, only to be forced to take on this very crucial but daunting role at that material time. He must have been both terrified and in shock too. Perhaps this was an answer to his prayers somewhat.

So, you child of God or you wanting to be a child of God by now; remember that you may find yourself in situations that have no apparent glory due to no fault or choice of yours. You never know what God Has Planned. Just be willing to obey His Voice. Simon could have said no, resisted and probably gotten himself killed for nothing.

Again it is a great lesson to learn – that although you may pray and wait too long (in your own opinion) for an answer; your answer may be just around the corner. Think hard, do not give up; if you do, you will miss the answer. This is faith at work too.

Your answer may well have been given at the very start (Daniel 10:12-13) but held up by the dark forces of this world; the principalities and powers of darkness in the heavenly places and here on earth.

Fear not; do not give up. For, our battle is not against flesh and blood (Ephesians 6:12). Jesus Christ Answers prayers. Be diligent; and He is surely, a trustworthy rewarder of those who diligently seek Him (Hebrews 11:6) without fainting. Pray ceaselessly and persevere. You are not forgotten at all; satan lies and deceives.

Well, I am exploring and writing about Jesus Christ, a man God, God in and as man. The Son of God, Son of Man, Sent of God, to die for you and for me, on the cross. The experience of a most gruesome journey, to a most gruesome and horrendous death.

Jesus Christ was eventually led to the place of the Skull (Golgotha) on Calvary (Mount). There, with more beatings, taunting, crying out in mockery, that He should save Himself (after all He said He was the Saviour King, one greater than a prophet); especially having performed so many miracles etc., He was tortured relentlessly. Jesus Christ did not give up. He stood firm, took it all and bore it all, in obedience to the Vision (Luke 23:26-55). He is the Lord God Almighty (1 Corinthians 8:5-7).

Jesus was thirsty and well "low, down". He was given wine vinegar on a sponge held up to His lips for drink (Mark 15:35-37). This was after being nailed to the cross. Please let my reader understand that you may cringe like me, whilst reading or letting this soak in. But, do remember that in those days, there were no fancy, lovely looking smooth nails that smoothly goes into wood. They must have been very rough nails that would take more flesh into the body to go through eventually, at the very least.

The pain He must have been in is inexplicable. No wonder He had Cried out asking why the Father had forsaken Him (Mark 15:33-35).

So, are you feeling like that today, did you feel that way yesterday, you may well feel like that tomorrow or the day after; take heart. Follow after the example of Jesus Christ. He Will see you through. He understands. However, if you suffer not for the sake of righteousness, even for the sake of Jesus Christ and faith in Him, you suffer but in vain (1 Peter 2:18-25).

So, whatever it is you are doing, if you are frustrated and can see no way out, you must not give up. Cry out nevertheless for His Help. Still no answer? Do not give up; but cry to Jesus for Help. Jesus Christ will make a way for you. Trust fully in Him. There is no other secure help anywhere else. Really, only Jesus Can Save. In no other name is there salvation (Acts 4:11-13).

The burden of our sins (the whole world) was laid upon Jesus Christ in one period only (of history). God let Him go, in order to complete the sacrifice. God Sacrificed His one and only Son, like Abraham's example mentioned earlier, but only this time, the real and final SACRIFICE for the salvation of humanity (for those who will believe). The Father watched and stood by as the Son died. But the Father had a Plan. God Knew beforehand that this sacrifice was to overcome and overpower satan in Great Victory.

Even having committed His spirit to God and died, they still pierced His side with a spear (John 19:33-35); blood and water gushed out. As if to make sure He died properly and never woke up again, He was brutalised right through unto death and after. However, suddenly, day turned to night; a sure sign that His was no cheap ordinary death. One of those officers present at His crucifixion declared that surely, He was truly the Son of the Most High Living God (Matthew 27:50-56).

We must not forget that Jesus Christ was offered in place of a criminal in prison, Barabbas, an insurrectionist, a rebel, he was chosen to be freed from prison; Jesus Christ was given up for death.

The people overwhelmingly opted to free Barabbas (Matthew 27:17-22). So what has changed. Jeremiah the Prophet was subjected to evil (Jeremiah 20:2; 35:15-17), like many of the fathers of faith before us and even in places around the world today. Jesus was taunted by one of the two thieves crucified on each side of Him. Oh what suffering, what a price that was paid for our salvation.

Please take the time to meditate on this sacrifice par excellence. Such sacrificial love. Take heart therefore in whatever you are facing today as a believer, follower of Jesus Christ. Your suffering will never be in vain, rather, it is pleasing unto God when you suffer for the sake of the Faith. Jesus Christ prepares us in His Word that we would be persecuted – taken before councils, flogged, etc. My dear reader, are you ready?

On the Third Day,
Jesus Christ Rose Again...

Jesus Christ had told His disciples that He would Rise on the third day, having prophesied of His Resurrection (Luke 24:6-8), Ascension and the Coming of the Holy Spirit whom He Would Send from Heaven. This is why He had told them not to sorrow over His having to go to the Father from whence He would Send the Holy Spirit. Did they believe Him though (Luke 24:11-12))? That is another matter entirely.

As promised, on the third day, Jesus Christ Rose again according to the Holy Scriptures (Luke 24). Although they foreknew this would happen, they were so much despondent that their "so-called" Saviour had died as He did and their faith shook. Despite having told them before hand that He Would Rise again on the third day, many were still very surprised indeed if not all of them, when He actually Rose again, even according to the Law of Moses, Prophets and the Psalms (Luke24:44). Dear reader, how much more certain can we be? Jesus Himself referenced His Being, even from the Old Testament. Do not be deceived.

Spectacularly, Thomas the Apostle had declared that unless he saw Jesus with his own eyes and touched Him and saw and touched his wounds, he would not believe. Well, Jesus let him. After all, the others had thought they saw a ghost when Jesus appeared to them (Luke 24:36-42). Thomas broke down and extolled the Great God in Jesus Christ, ashamed of his unbelief. But now, having had his request met, he believed. Jesus said Blessed are those who believed without evidence (John20:24-29).

Thomas bowed to Jesus Christ and acknowledged with honour, the Great Father in Jesus Christ, our God and King. Amen. How disappointing and painful to Arise and still find unbelief in His own disciples. Yet, what patience, what loving kindness and tenderness, to still see them through unto believing.

A note, worthy of mention is that when Mary tried to hold onto Him when she saw that it was the Lord who had Arisen, Jesus prevented her, saying, He had not yet returned to the Father (John20:17-18).

In the presence of witnesses and at the appointed time, Jesus Revealed Himself to Many (1 Corinthians 15:5-7). He Ascended unto Heaven and was taken up in a cloud, having promised them that He would return (Luke 24:50-51). We have His Sure Word on this; and for this reason, like many others before me, I am writing to prepare not just myself, but you the reader, for the second coming of our Lord Jesus Christ.

Your sincere appreciation and understanding of the Supreme Sacrifice in and of Love is a very crucial aspect of faith in Jesus Christ. So, do you believe this sacrifice? You will and must know in your heart. Your spirit will respond to this message. If this is the case, you are Blessed. If not, keep on, regardless; keep on reading. I assure you that all whom the Lord Wills unto Himself shall respond and experience the Joy of this Divine Sacrifice.

Love...

I cannot get away from this subject of love. I am Inspired and Compelled to open up this Love of and for God to you the reader some more. Let us go into the attributes of love. Many say that love is the answer; but they revel wantonly, wilfully and carelessly, in lustful, manipulative behaviour, which is laden with witchcraft, sorceries and all manners of idolatry. They present this to all and sundry as love, thereby causing many to deviate from and ultimately abandon the true faith in Jesus Christ.

They speak with "nice" soft voices and seduce their preys with skilful ease. Such people embrace hatred within; and they are often damaged beyond repairs. They hate with such a passion and have their egos well enriched with lustful pleasures, which they will not want to give up. They pretend that their lusts are "no big deal". God does not mind anyway. God goes for far more important, bigger things, etc.

Well, let me assure you; a great ocean begins with the little droplets, then trickles, of water. The very things you consider no big deal are the very building blocks that help to root and prove your faith. The practitioners of this strange but common behaviour (that they so much want for you to believe is love) "hate" with such a passion that they easily transfer their hatred to the weak and heavily laden. They draw the weak into diverse perversions.

Jesus Christ is saying to you who are trapped in such teachings and practices to come out of them now; today, not tomorrow. Now. They teach you about a love that knows no pain. They feign a love that is full of roses and is always red and or pink and or blue and or royal purple. Do not be deceived. Love is separate from lust. They even teach you women to seduce your own husbands and say this is ok, as God Himself Gave you the gift of seductive ability. What perversion; lies from the pits of hell. Satan is the original seducer and the father of all liars and practitioners of evil.

When husbands and wives have to seduce each other, they are in the world not in Jesus Christ. When you seduce each other and out in the world others seduce you, how will you cope, when you claim to be in Jesus Christ? It is no wonder that our marriages increasingly break up. The truth is bitter to us; we pretend this is not the case. We practice political and other fake correctness.

We often live, not in Christ to gratify the Spirit nature; but mostly, in sin to gratify the sinful nature. We claim love for the Lord but profane His name (Ezekiel 13:19) freely with our practices of worldliness, rooted very deeply in our so-called church gatherings.

When are we going to wake up? We assume that He who made the senses cannot see, hear and or deal with our frivolities and deceptions? Not so, He is patient with us, in anguish of love over us for not loving Him and obeying Him, to follow after the Way of Love, via a Faith that lives Holy.

Okay, so what is love I hear you say? All the bashing etc.? No, it is not for bashing that I write; but for awakening a revival in your spirit man. When righteousness is preached, the so-called believers are quickest to judge and declare the arrival of Bible bashing (I do not see any such words in my copy of the Holy Scriptures). It is very much fashionable now to be "born again"; yet, on closer observation, most are born against the word of God and revel in wanton disobedience to the Author of Life.

I have asked many people who claim to know God and are teaching many others about God and Love etc. and they came up with all sorts of worldly illusions of lust, rather than the love of God. In their diverse, eloquent definitions of love and its attributes, what I hear is about the sharing of idols (gifts they call them – rings, etc. etc.)

in the name of Love. They go on and on about non-Biblical issues, whims and caprices to be mutually satisfied by the practitioners of this their strange type of love.

When I ask further where in God's Word such is encouraged as love, I meet with great hostility and grief, laden with allegations of my arrogance and harshness and falsehood etc. With great eloquence, they break down love to several parts as if God can be broken down and teach itching ears freely (as love) what is not in the Holy Scriptures, rather the fanciful words of human understanding and knowledge (not of God). Whereas, the Bible urges that we do not lean upon our own understanding (Proverbs 3:5).

Well, thanks be unto God in Jesus Christ, the Wisdom and Power of God, who is the Way, Truth and Life; and in whom true Love is vested in full and excellently. Amen. Now, dear reader, be fully assured of this.

Also, feel free to check it out fully and freely in the Holy Scriptures too. Love is espoused in the Holy Scriptures profoundly in the Book of 1 Corinthians 13. Let me say that a relationship of love must be established between any true believer/follower of Jesus Christ and Jesus Christ Himself. He paid the ultimate price in a most sacrificial and unselfish way and it is only in Him that we can come into the knowledge and true understanding of Love. He alone can teach us to love.

No one can buy a horse or just find one in the woods and ride it home or just receive a gift of one and do likewise (just like that). You do not just immediately jump on a horse and ride it away. There must be a breaking in process. Even for a car, there is a breaking in process before it is said to be safe and smooth for driving although it may be brand new. This process is a getting-to-know (familiarisation) process.

The horse and the new rider (or the car and new owner/driver) must get to know each other.

After that, suitability is established in terms of what the driver needs and feels comfortable with; and in the case of the horse, a relationship is struck. The two parties may not "gel" (work well together). Hence, the need to try out how well they work together. This is the first step in any relationship that is being built. There will be teething problems as in marriage when two different people come together as one.

This process, if given the right and due attention, can lead to a very special relationship. Then and only then can the rider/owner receive the respect and obedience of the horse (and the best service from the car). The horse/car would perform for the owner and respond to training/discipline, guidance etc. and diligent care as the case may be.

Without getting carried away, I am writing about love now; and the need for a willingness to give and take and keep working to keep love flowing. Love is not what most people think it is. Now, it is established that the horse/car (to continue my example) belongs to the owner. The owner on the other hand values the horse/car and does his best to cater for (feed, groom, train and care for as the case may be) the possession.

Regardless of whether the horse/car wins trophies, most owners love them anyway. The key to mutual sacrificial loving is in being yoked to the object of love.

In this case, I am writing about the followers and believers of Jesus Christ being yoked with Him (Matthew 11:28-30). True love, when established between you and Jesus Christ, will spill into any relationships within marriage etc. wherever you go. To learn to be holy and perfect as God is in Jesus Christ is to be very closely in tune with God's Holy Spirit. Likewise, to worship Him in spirit and in truth. This is what He requires of us. For man, this may seem impossible. With God, all things are possible.

Many out there, in responsible positions of trust over many others (families, men, women, children etc.) teach that you cannot keep the Commandments of God or meet the Standards of God. I do not see that in the Holy Scriptures. They tell you not to bother trying because they failed. They assure you that you will fail and can never meet up with God's standards. When caught out, they make excuses and say God only looks upon the heart.

If God only looks upon your heart, God would not ask that you present your body to Him, holy and that is your spiritual act of sacrifice (Romans 12:1). Be not deceived; God cannot be mocked. We shall all reap whatsoever we sow (Galatians 6:6-8).

If you strongly desire the love of God, then likewise, strongly desire and be determined to obey God's Commandments, Instructions and His Words. Trustworthy, Inspired servants, have been faithful. So, we have our Holy Scriptures. Do not allow anyone to present sculptured scriptures to you, no matter how lovely it is presented. That is idolatry. A curse is upon anyone who adds to or takes away from the Word of God (Revelations 22:18-19). God hates that. Obey the Word.

Love and the Commandments...

Jesus Christ said over and over again throughout the Holy Scriptures that the proof of love for Him is to obey His Commandments. This is unchanging unto eternity.

The story of God's love for humanity begins with the very creation of man in God's image (Genesis 1). Then He created woman from the side of man (rib taken whilst man slept). So, with man and woman (his helpmate), God Revealed Himself as a loving father and put man in charge of creation (even in the Garden of Eden before the fall of man).

God saw that man was alone and declared that it is not good for man to be alone. So, God created woman for man as a helpmate (Genesis 2) and Blessed us with a special relationship also based on love (rooted originally in love).

However, man did not live up to expectation and soon fell out of favour through his inability to obey God's Instructions, laws and commands (Genesis 3). Man of course fell as a result of the woman's choice to disobey God and encourage man to do the same. Man responded. The root of man's disobedience is entwined with satan's cunning and influence on the woman (the weaker vessel), seeing and knowing that the woman is weaker somehow or other.

This lack of love for God is very evident in our society today (including amongst so-called believers). The choices men and women make in coming together as husbands and wives often reflect the pattern of the original fall. Such is the prevalence of disobedience in our world today that it is almost impossible to sustain a marriage to its conclusive end. We make our own laws and opt for equality, political correctness etc., to our own ruin.

The institution of marriage is holy unto the Lord. It is the only example that God likens the relationship Jesus Christ has with His Church to (Ephesians 5). Marriage has become increasingly farcical in our world today, especially, amongst those who claim to walk in the Holy Name of Jesus Christ.

It is worth meditating on this for God's Wisdom to be made manifest unto the true followers of Christ Jesus.

Man is primarily entrusted with God's Word and His Will; and as the leader designate, in the discharging of human responsibilities to God. Right through God's Word, this is evident. What many cannot understand is that God's Ways and Thoughts are not like ours (Isaiah 55:8-9) at all and in the name of freeing woman from man's leadership and domination (Genesis 2:18-25, 3:16; Ephesians 5:22-24), we have gone away from the Holy Word and also from God's laid down Structures for our existence.

The results are very clearly seen in our daily world today. We have deviated from the Standard by which we ought to take dominion over the creation (Genesis 1:28). The universe, our world has been short changed like a faulty circuit and we are increasingly experiencing the attending malaise of a vast and diverse extent/nature, globally. For this, God's judgment is certain (Revelation 11:18).

That God put man in charge has now become a target for manipulation. This does not mean that woman is irrelevant at all; nor should it be treated as such. Woman is not in any way irrelevant; nor is woman for beating and enslavement in the way of the world. No, not so at all. Likewise, in reacting to the authority of man, man is neither for receiving such treatment from woman. Love is the answer. God's Love will right all wrongs if allowed to prevail. To follow God's Will and obey, is the answer to this growing menace and global madness.

It takes Godly wisdom (1 Kings 3; Daniel 5:11-15; Romans 11:33; 1 Corinthians 1:18-31) and the Leading of the Holy Spirit for mankind to know how to apply Godly Wisdom, in learning and teaching about the structures of God, even in love. In Godly living, there has to be a head and God chose man for this purpose. This is not something to be envied by woman or hated etc.; nor is it something to be taken out of context by man, so as to want to ride on the woman's back, in the name of submission.

You, mister man, must firstly submit to God; and your woman will be drawn to submit to your authority, if she is of God's stock. Man must be Godly in disposition and fully responsible to care for the "garden". Yes, God gave woman to help man to discharge his responsibilities and leadership roles. It is very important to grasp this to be able to understand the love of God ; and now, we must submit to Him as a woman onto God and her husband.

Men must lead by example. However, it is not for the woman to capitalise on man's mistakes so as to undermine him either. A wise woman will apply the wisdom of God as laid out in the Holy Scriptures even in the example of Sarah, the wife of Abraham, to help her husband to lead as best as he could (1 Peter 3:1-7). A woman of God will be a good help mate and not usurp the man's authority. She will also bring up her sons in the spirit of man and not feminise them as we see so much today. Man and woman both must persevere in love and give a good example unto the children so they can honour our God.

God in Jesus Christ is the husband of the Church and is coming back for a bride without blemish (Ephesians 5:27; Colossians 1:22). So, let no one be in doubt that in Truth, God's Word says that without faith, no man can please God, without holiness no man will see the Lord (Hebrews 11:6, 12:14). The goal of followers of Jesus Christ is to ultimately enter into His Heavenly Kingdom (new Jerusalem) where shall see Him face to face. Love is the only Way;

Jesus Christ is His Name. He is the Lord God Almighty; and as God is Love, He, being God, is Love. Amen.

More on Love…

My dear reader, Love is too important not to be fully investigated in any matter of faith. Love is central to all and in all that has to do with God. Jesus Christ did not mince words in this matter at all. We are reminded over and over again, all through the Holy Scriptures, about the Power of Love (2 Timothy 1:6-8) and the consequences of anything (thoughts, words or deeds) devoid of love. It is love that would answer all of your problems in life and I assure you that you will not regret getting deeper and deeper with me on this matter at all. Rather, you will be very Blessed.

Since the goal of the sincere follower (believer in or follower) of Jesus Christ is God, we understand fully and absolutely that God is love. Jesus Christ is God; and we must likewise know that He is Love. We therefore have a great assurance in knowing that, to have our goal as and in Love, is a most worthy cause to put all we have into; even as we learn and put love into practice/action.

The Holy Scriptures make very clear the importance of faith as a prerequisite for pleasing God; in fact, without faith no one can please God. It is made also abundantly clear that the only thing that really matters is faith that works through Love in all of our experience of God in life (Galatians 5:6). If you want more love, you must start to give and increase in giving love. If you do not know love or how to give love, ask, seek and knock; you shall receive (find) and love shall be opened unto you in Jesus' Name (Luke 11:9-11). Amen.

Nevertheless, I have made very clear that the fear of God is a must in order to learn wisdom. Without wisdom there is no way that anyone can really learn anything about a God who Himself is infinitely all Wise; and only reveals Himself to those who fear Him.

All of these go together: the fear of God, faith, hope, love. It is most essential in realising this goal, to learn about, meditate upon and master the Way of Love.

The Way of Love cannot be devoid of the fear of God and faith; faith cannot be devoid of hope; and Love feeds into both; and is the only Power that drives them all into effectiveness. Although love is assuredly the greatest of all; they cannot but work and walk together as one in all, in order to be effective and to be able to reach the ultimate goal of entering into the Kingdom of God.

Jesus Christ is the Light of all the world according to the Holy Scriptures (John 9:5) which also emphatically state that God is Light and clothes Himself with Light as a garment (Psalm 104:2). Love is holy and pure. The more we learn about God, the closer we get towards love and the more Light is shed upon us. As we receive more Light into our lives, we shall get closer and nearer to God. As we do, we shall increase in the fear of God. The fear of God being the beginning of wisdom (without which we cannot get close to God), will draw God closer to us. So, let Light in. Let Him in. His name is Jesus.

Consequently, darkness will increasingly flee from our lives. Light exposes darkness as love increases in us; because, love is light. This is a scary process for many humans; and do not be surprised that when you meet love you will shudder with fear within. This is satan's device to make you feel confused about love; since, had you known love, you would recognise that there is the fear of God in love. I am not dealing with the issue of the fear of man right here, in this minute.

God is the one to truly Dread for He is the Dreadful one. No need to fear where there is none to fear (Psalm 14:5; Isaiah 8:12-13; Hebrews 10:31). When some quote the Bible for you and say that perfect love casts out all fear (1 John 4:18), this is not talking about casting out the fear of God. As you increase in the fear of God,

Love will increase in you and you will learn to fear God the more. As you fear God the more, your fear of what mankind can do to you, will drastically and dramatically reduce. This is what is meant by, Perfect Love casting out all fear. Remember too, that, the fear of God is the beginning of wisdom for you. Fear God.

Let me clarify further. Your neighbours cat may terrify other neighbours until one of them gets a dog. When this happens the dog becomes the boss. The next neighbour may then get a wilder dog which the previous one's dog cannot match. I am saying that all fear will bow when the One to be Dreaded fills you with Love.

Then, the Bible says that even your enemies will bow at your feet (Isaiah 49:23, 60:14). The elephant is very elegant and very big but is not considered as the king of the animals. That post is reserved for the lion. There is a reason for this. Where the dog is barking and harassing the lower, lesser, weaker animals, the arrival of the cub lion changes all that quickly, just in case the lioness is around.

I have seen many a big bully turn into a "pussycat" when a smaller child stands up to him or her in the class in front of the others. In the small fight that ensued earlier, the big bully actually slipped and fell with a bang. There is no copping out, or excusing the fact. The bully was clearly smashed down in the eyes of observers; and in the confusion of all the noise and hailing of the younger, smaller child, the big bully lost face for good.

Our God is not a bully but when He is with you, when on your side, the dread of you falls upon your enemies. We see clear examples in the children of Israel (Exodus 1:12; Numbers 22:3).

I am however writing about the Power of Love. Love is Supreme. Love demolishes every satanic stronghold in your life when you dare to believe. Love is Light. Love is a Healing Force. Love is not just gentle. Love is a devastating force when it chooses to be. Love is not just about being soft and gentle; Love can be very forceful too, for Love is Powerful beyond measure. Love builds but can also tear down. Do you doubt this? Please read some of Jesus Christ's Words again in the New Testament. I will encourage you to read the Prophets and the Law too. God Sent His Word for you.

Everywhere love goes and is welcome sincerely, love flows actively and healing flows too (Malachi 4:2). Love is the Power of God for all life. Wherever Jesus Christ went (Acts 10:37-39), He was doing Good (good works abound to prove love's presence). How true this is when we get to study and understand the very nature and essence of Love. Remember however, faith is very crucial to the workings of love. For Jesus Christ Himself could not do much in His own hometown because of their lack of faith (Mark 6:3-5)John 12:37; Hebrews 3:19).

There is absolutely nothing impossible for love, for God is Love; and we must remember this right through the study and practice of love in our daily lives and walk with God as followers (and would be followers) of Jesus Christ. Anybody truly in search of/after/for Truth, who is willing to go for the Way of Love as laid down as a Standard for all in the Holy Scriptures will eventually meet with our Lord Jesus Christ by Divine Revelation.

It is written that if those who are not followers of Jesus Christ (by nature) live lives that prove and or reflect that the Laws of God in Jesus Christ are written on their hearts, they will be judged accordingly (as though they were in Christ Jesus). This is clearly laid out in the Book of Romans, Chapter 2:12-16, as well as the consequences of not doing so. However, here, we are dealing with the issues around love and loving (for now).

Let us examine the words of our Lord Jesus Christ that those who love Him must/will obey His Commandments. In so doing, let us remember that Jesus Christ spoke in parables. Therefore, I invite you my reader to open your mind fully right now (and or check if indeed you are allowing yourself to flow accordingly) and be fully relaxed and at ease.

There is the saying that anything worth doing is worth doing well. The results/rewards of your willingness to receive the Truth of Love will change your life forever (for good), if you are willing to be disciplined in your approach to learning God's Love.

In deeply meditating on God's Word, I learnt from the Holy Spirit's Counsel that the Commandments of God in Jesus Christ are what God gave to Moses as the Ten Commandments (in summary according to Deuteronomy 5:1-22). These were further elaborated upon in the (what are now called) Mosaic Laws (Leviticus). Again, the Ten Commandments are a summary of God's Laws. Our Lord Jesus Christ then revealed to us through His Holy Spirit, the "Executive Summary" in very simple and clear terms (Luke 10:27; John 13:34-35; Romans 13:8), referred to as the "New Commandment" to love one another as He Love(d)s us.

By loving one another as Jesus Christ love(d)s us, we prove to and show all men that we are His disciples (no other way, only if we love one another).

Jesus Christ went further to combine these in an extraordinary way in the "Greatest Commandment" (Matthew 22:34-40) that we must love the Lord our God with all our hearts, souls, minds, strength and power. This is regarded and seen right through the Holy Scriptures as the first and greatest commandment. Jesus Christ gave us a second, which He said was just like the first, that we must love our neighbour as ourselves.

Jesus Christ declared with all power and authority that all the Law and the Prophets hang on these two commandments.

It would appear that the writer is repeating some of these same issues over and over again. This is a deliberate effort as the Holy

Spirit of God is leading me, for the purpose of enabling everyone who has determined to take and get the best of this message to tap into and have the maximum potential/profit/opportunity to engage with the Holy Spirit in pure absolute Love.

Love changes lives. Love knows all things and sees all things. Love covers a multitude of sins. Love makes a way where there is no way. Love is revealing. Love is a revelation. All power is invested in love. God's Love is the power that Saves, Heals, Delivers and Blesses. At the end of all things including life, love alone possesses the power to Judge; and will do so Justly (1 Peter 2:22-24, 4:4-6; 2 Thessalonians 1:5-7; James 5:8-9; Acts 10:41-43).

I am so Blessed to recall in support of my exposition with regard to God's Love, the following, in the words in a verse of a song I remember and love so much from my childhood, "... God moves in a mysterious way, His Wonders to Perform ... He Plants His Footsteps in the sea ... and Rides upon the storm ... "; the song goes on somewhere to say that "... the bud may have a bitter taste ... but sweet will be the flower ... " (Songs of Praise). This excellently exemplifies Love – may be bitter to the taste when eating (learning and putting to practice), but sweet in reward (when fulfilled).

The bitterness is reminiscent of the other side of love, which is painful. Love can be sour too; and a sourness seen in the discipline aspect of love is shown possibly in the prophetic Revelations. When the Apostle John was told to eat the Scroll in the Book of Revelation, Chapter10:9-10, it tasted very sweet in his mouth but was very sour in his stomach. Therefore in love, there will be bitter, sour, as well as sweet (so love is made whole).

Yet the joy of God's Love is deep and made complete in love. Be prepared therefore my reader, to learn the Truth of Love. Amen. To learn the Way of Love is to know Life. The fear of God alone leads to the right mindset (disciplined approach) to appreciate and enter into the very nature, essence and covenant of Love.

Again, another part of the song I mentioned earlier says of God that " ... behind a frowning Providence, He hides a Smiling Face ... ". I do not know what the writer of this song (and of course many others) saw, but I tell you dear reader, that it is true that God is Good and His Mercies endure forevermore. Amen.

When the Scriptures state emphatically that our Lord Jesus Himself learnt obedience through the things He Suffered, this was clearly through faith (Hebrews 5). He Pleased God and found Favour so much so that the fullness of God's very Being Dwelt upon/with Him (Colossians 2:8-10). Surely, this was to show us how to draw near to God, so He Will draw near to us.

If you draw nearer to God (Hebrews 10:23-22), you will begin to know and learn His Commandments to enable you to know His Ways. Let me hereby link you up with God's Commandments as He Leads me right here.

More on Love and the Commandments...

If you truly love God or want to learn to do so, you shall:

1. Have no other gods before God (Deuteronomy 5:7)

No matter how clever you are, you may make excuses of all sorts, but I tell you that you are a slave to whatever you refuse to give up for the sake of following Jesus Christ. This may be your lustful youthful desire for jewellery, make-up, wealth (money), work, sex and sexy clothing, witchcraft, occult, freemasonry, homosexuality, lesbianism, masturbation, kinky sex, diverse perversions, men/women's clothing power, etc. You may deceive and mock only yourself; for God cannot be mocked. We shall all reap whatsoever we have sown.

Warning is available in Romans 1 and 2; also, 2 Timothy 3. So, you must repent willingly and earnestly seek after God's Help through Jesus Christ to receive forgiveness and empowerment of the Holy Spirit to enable you to live a Godly, Holy life, which is pleasing unto God. For you, this may seem impossible, but with God, all thing are possible; only believe. Dare to humble yourself and come to Jesus Christ. Accept His Sovereignty and Help and submit fully to Jesus Christ and be saved.

2. Not make for yourself an idol in the form of anything in Heaven above or in the waters below (Deuteronomy 5:8-10)

You shall not bow to them or worship them; for the Lord is a jealous God, punishing the children for the sin of the fathers to the third and fourth generations of those who hate Him, but showing love to a thousand generations of those who love Him and keep His Commandments.

Well, my previous words apply in this second scenario too (as the first). In addition, let my reader believe and not doubt that all of these apply today; and disobeying them, is why many people remain bound. Even without going to anyone for deliverance, if anyone is determined to follow God and begin to fully yield to Him by forsaking idols and idolatry, having no other gods, such will be saved as they cry out to God through Jesus Christ.

Many have been thus delivered. However, for my readers, you must know that you are in sin and want God to save you through Jesus Christ. For, only Jesus Christ can save.

Disobedience is the foundation, root and greatest of all sin (disobedience against God's Word) – i.e. (y)ours and my choice(s) not to obey God's Word and His Commandments. Let no one deceive you about this grace and New Testament dispensation, where you are told that all is well. As a result, sin abounds all the more, as proof that all is not well at all.

God's Spirit hates sin (Psalm 5:4-6). If you live in and continue in sin, gratifying the sinful nature, you will surely go to hell (1 Corinthians 6:9-10; Galatians 5:20-22; Ephesians 5:4-6). Your only hope is to repent and allow Jesus Christ to enter into your life to enable His Holy Spirit to renew your mind and Help you to live for God in Jesus Christ. There is no other hope for the salvation of anyone; only Jesus can save you (Acts 4:12). The words of this second commandment are very practically self revealing as all others.

3. **Not misuse the Name of the Lord your God, for the Lord will not hold anyone guiltless who misuses His Name (Deuteronomy 5:11)**

We use the Holy Name of God, even in Christ Jesus as we like. With insincerity in our hearts, we call on Him. We do not honour Him as required and as He Deserves. We even use slangs with regard to the Holy Name. Oh God, we say, when we are not even thinking of Him. Oh gosh, sometimes, even when nothing Godly is at stake. This is self-explicit and we must take care to Hallow His Holy Name. There is no compromising the Name of God. We must not take the Lord's Name in vain.

4. **Remember the Sabbath Day to keep it Holy (Deuteronomy 5:12)**

Six days you shall labour and do all your work but the seventh day is a Sabbath to the Lord your God. On it, you shall do no work, neither you nor your son or daughter nor your man/maidservant; nor your animals, nor the aliens within your gates. For in six days the Lord made the Heavens and the earth, the sea and all that is in them, but He Rested on the Seventh Day. Therefore, the Lord Blessed the Sabbath Day and made it holy. Again, the above is very self-explicit.

However, in the New Testament, we have the privilege to enter into Jesus Christ Himself, who is the Sabbath (Mark 2:27-28). Some hold one day as holy, others all days (Romans 14:4-6), the important thing is to be in the Spirit of the Sabbath, which is holy and ensure that you are in the Rest of the Lord God Almighty. So, some say the Sabbath is Sunday. Others say it is Saturday. Others hold that all days are and or can be the Sabbath day.

The Holy Scriptures show me that as long as we are not wicked (2 Chronicles 7:14); and we follow after faith that works through love, we shall be safe in Christ Jesus, having entered into His Sabbath. Jesus Christ Himself is the Sabbath. For the world can harass us and frustrate us even from our Sunday/Saturday worship (Sabbath). However, the world cannot take away our Sabbath in the Lord Jesus Christ on a day to day basis. Amen.

Myself, I respect all and judge none as per which day to keep Holy as long as I choose to enter the Lord's Rest daily, personally. Each must take a faith decision and let the Holy Spirit Lead. Amen.

5. Honour your father and mother, so that you may live long in the land that the Lord your God is giving you (Deuteronomy 5:16)

It is no wonder that as a fulfilment of the Holy Scriptures, we live in a very largely and increasingly godless world today (2 Timothy 3:1-9). Mutual respect is rare; as is honour for parents. Not even in schools is there respect/honour for teachers anymore. Respect/honour for elders is as rare as that for parents/teachers too. The commandment is very clear.

In the Book of Timothy and Titus, Paul the Apostle also instructed how we ought to relate to one another as children of God. In Ephesians also, we are encouraged in terms of how husbands and wives, parents and children ought to relate to each other too. If only we would be obedient to God's Word and Commandments, how much better our lives would be.

Those of us who claim to be born again (of the Spirit and Water), in the Holy Name of Jesus Christ and filled with His Holy Spirit ought to be particularly mindful to not profane His Holy Name, nor bring God' Name in Christ Jesus into disrepute. Alas, we are especially guilty of not holding the forte, even though we know more than all else that the Coming of our Lord Jesus Christ is near (Luke 21:5-38).

In the Name of God the Father, Son and Holy Spirit, all His Own are baptised (Matthew 28:8-20). As a result, we more than any other(s) ought to be a reflection of His very being. To those being saved, we ought to be as a sweet aroma of Jesus Christ; whilst to those perishing, a stench (2 Corinthians 2:14-16). Often, we want to be the opposite with the latter, to please them, against the Word of God. When we dishonour God in Christ Jesus through our disobedience and by not loving one another, the world dishonour and profane His Name because of us (Ezekiel 36:19-21).

We have a duty and a responsibility unto God to obey His Commandments and to love one another as He Commanded us. Only by the latter would the world recognise us as His disciples. Otherwise, we deceive ourselves, live a lie and the Truth is not in us. Anyone who says they love God and hates their brother is a murderer according to the Holy Scriptures (1 John 3:15; 1 John 4:20). Yet, the Word of God is fully against murder.

6. Not kill another human being (Deuteronomy 5:17)

We have been commanded not to kill/murder another human being (person). We are not permitted to take another person's life. This commandment is very self-explicit. There are serious consequences for disobedience. Murder is committed in diverse ways; not just as humans would like to think.

You can kill with your mouth too. Also, by abortion, via racism and other forms of wickedness etc. God is just and will punish according to His Wisdom in the final analysis. When you deprive others or withhold their dues unjustly; and their lives are affected so much so as to cause them to become ill and eventually lose their lives, although you may not be punished by man, God is the ultimate Judge. You will surely pay.

7. Not commit adultery (Deuteronomy 5:18)

We are encouraged throughout the Word of God to refrain from sexual immorality (Romans 13:13; 1 Corinthians 6:10-20) and this includes not engaging in (thoughts, words and deeds) acts of a sexual nature against another person's wife/husband. We must also not engage in such against another person before marriage either (fornication).

We are to honour God in Christ Jesus with our bodies. If we are not called unto celibacy (and this is a gift, we have to be given otherwise we cannot do this), we are to marry our own wives or husbands, if we cannot hold ourselves. There is no use burning with passion (1 Corinthians 7:9, 36). So, get married. Although it is better according to the Scriptures not to marry (1 Corinthians 7:1); again, this has to be God-led, Granted as a gift.

When married, we are not to dishonour the marital bed by engaging in (sinful) sexual activities (in thoughts, words, deeds) within or outside the marriage. Outside, meaning the obvious interaction with any other than the spouse. Within, meaning the less obvious engagement in passionate lusts like pagans, revelling in diverse perversions that are unholy and lead to evil.

God is Holy and the consequences of disobedience are very much evident regardless of who we are. Our body is the temple of the Living God and we are to present our body to Him as our spiritual act of sacrifice as holy and acceptable offering unto Him (Romans 12:1).

All other sins we commit are outside our body but sexual sins are directly against our body, the temple of the Living God. We cannot do as we please with our body. Many do not consider this today at all and when told they get very hateful and angry against the servant of God.

8. Not steal (Deuteronomy 5:19)

We are not to take another person's belonging and or possession unto ourselves without their permission (whether by force or not). This is sinful. It is not alright even to steal from parents. Some steal from work, etc. Stealing is stealing.

What is not yours must not be taken without the owner's permission (not by stealth, bullying nor forcefully). Greed, avarice etc., often borne out of godlessness without contentment as against godliness with contentment, play a part. Always wanting what others have is a part of it (1 Timothy 6:6).

9. Not give false testimonies against your neighbour(s) (Deuteronomy 5:20)

To give false testimonies against neighbours is sinful (even as it amounts to lying). To gang up and speak and or proffer lies against a neighbour is not Godly and is evil and sinful. To then even be prepared to stand up in court to do so is grievous evil, sinful unto God. We must not do this. When others are planning such evil and engage in mockery etc., where do you stand? Consider Psalm 1 very carefully. God sees all.

10. Not covet your neighbours' home; not his wife (or husband), man/maidservant, ox, donkey, or anything belonging to your neighbour (Deuteronomy 5:21)

Not being satisfied with what we have, despite God's Counsel (that Godliness with contentment is great gain), is sinful unto God. Covetousness leads to stealing, selfish abuse of authority, murders, etc. It is not only when the offence is committed that we sin. Even the thought to do it or want it is as sinful as engaging directly in the sin itself. Jesus said that it is our lustful, worldly desires that cause fights, strife and wars amongst us. These come from lustful desires battling within our souls (James 4:1-4).

The writer is being Blessed to touch on this subject of the Ten Commandments of God. How ancient; yet, so righteous. They bring healing to us when we are willing to be determined to leave no stones unturned in obeying them, as no one will see the Lord without holiness. If you do not obey the Commandments of God, yet you claim to be under God's Grace, under Jesus Christ, you cannot but live in wilful sin. So, do not be deceived. Strive to refrain from sin always. The wages of sin of course, is death (Romans 6:23).

I pray that God in Jesus Christ Touches all hearts reading this message in its fullness to Supernaturally Help us to refrain from sin, as a choice, even as we draw closer to God in Jesus Christ.

Also, even as we strive to be holy and perfect, even as God is Holy and Perfect in Christ Jesus, may our lives become increasingly acceptable and worthy of Him who sacrificed Himself for us and called us unto Himself. Amen.

Love and fear for God will engage us in willingly submitting to His Authority and wanting to choose to obey His Words and Commandments. Love and fear for God will lead us to want to study His Word and listen for His Holy Spirit's Counsel (John 1:26) and meditate on these; so much so that, as we put these to use and practice in our lives day to day, we would strive to be more like Jesus Christ, in thoughts, words and deeds (1 John 4:16-18).

We then position ourselves strategically, to yield/submit fully and absolutely to His Transforming Holy Spirit (James 4:1,7; Romans 12:2;

2 Corinthians 3:18), who leads us into all truth and all righteousness forever and ever in Christ Jesus' Holy Name, Amen.

It is this same love that enables us to fear and love Him deeper every day with all our hearts, minds, souls, bodies and power. Only then can we effectively begin to enjoy His Word.

To enter into the Joy of living a life in Jesus Christ is to get deeper into His Word and really begin to meditate and reflect on His Teachings; enough to apply in daily living with regard to our neighbours. Now remember who is your neighbour? Jesus Christ answered such a question with the words that whomsoever is within your power/reach to help or extend mercy to, is your neighbour (Luke 10:27).

Not just your friends/family and or next-door neighbour alone. The Word of God also says that if it is within your power/reach to help someone, do not deny him/her. So, now that you know your neighbour and the true essence of love? Do you love me?

Husbands, wives, do you love each other? Brothers and sisters, friend(s) and foes, do you love each other? Do you love each other? Do you love your father/mother? Am I your neighbour? Do you love your enemy(ies)? This is the true test of your faith. Not only to love one another but to prove your love for Jesus Christ in not just forgiving each other but your enemy(ies) too (with the Love of God in Jesus Christ). Jesus said, if you do good to those who love you really you have done nothing spectacular. But if you love your enemy(ies) and when they are hungry/thirsty, you give them food/drink then your Father in Heaven will truly be pleased with you, knowing for sure that you are truly in love with Him and will obey Him fully and truly in everything (Luke 6:27-36).

However, when the simple foundations of faith are still a bone of contention between you and the servant of God, then you, who should by now, be teaching others, you need milk not solid food or even meat (Hebrews 5:13-14). By now we should put aside the elementary teachings (not ignore or discard them) for they are the building blocks onto solid food (for the mature). The mature through constant use have become acquainted with solid food.

This is for your edification; not to put you down, my dearly beloved. That you may know how deep, rich and real, is the depth of God's love for you in and through Jesus Christ, Son of God, Everlasting Father, King of Kings, Prince of Peace (Ephesians 3:17-19). Amen.

Before we can learn to live and love our neighbours as ourselves, first we must fear God and love Him deeply. God reveals our hearts to us as we draw closer to Him and we then see how we can make changes in terms of how we relate to our neighbours. Hence, the Scripture that says to draw near to God and He Will draw near to you (James 4:8).

The Counsel of God in Jesus Christ to do unto others as we would have them do unto us (Matthew 7:2-5, 12) is rooted in this principle and helps us to choose to do good to our neighbours as we would not want them to do otherwise to us. Gradually, we learn that it is better and even more profitable to love our enemies as Jesus Christ Himself Counselled us to do in His Written Word. Amen.

I am not and do not in anyway suggest that this is easy. Only the Holy Spirit makes it bearable (2 Timothy 1:13-14) for us to live for God in faith and holiness that works through love. We however must be willing and ready in full submission and with reverent fear, for God to Lead us through His Holy Spirit as sons.

Increasing in Love...
Love reveals that sin is sweet but Masked...

For the above reason, we need love increasingly, to help us in judging ourselves, based on the aspects of love. This will help us to continually assess and test ourselves; and see that we are still in the faith (2 Corinthians 13:5). Satan is crafty like a fox and draws us with the "idols" of our affections, in our lives, until he gets a good grip, like a python and then he begins to crush us until he swallows us up in death, in sin unto eternal damnation. Sin leads unto death; living for Jesus leads unto life.

The Bible says clearly that the wages of sin is death but the gift of God is Eternal Life, even through Christ Jesus (Romans 6:23). Amen. Therefore, we can avoid the former, i.e. the way that seems right to us which is sweet but leads only onto death (Proverbs 14:12; 16:25). We have a choice though; but we are urged in the Word of God to choose life, even eternal life (Deuteronomy 30:19). To do this, love is the only way/answer, even as we prove our love by obeying the commandments and not just being hearers, but doers of the Word (Romans 2:13; James 1:22-24; Matthew 7:24-26).

No matter how gifted I am or you are, no matter how blessed by God (remember Lucifer was an archangel of God and very blessed), without love, we are nothing, we are empty and of no good to anyone, not to God and not to any man. Then we are just empty vessels making noise(s), an irritation onto God basically.

In the first letter of Paul the Apostle to the Corinthians, Chapter 13, the Holy God in Jesus Christ Blessed us to know some of the concise but powerful attributes of love that are life-changing for anyone who dares to put them to practice. Just before the exposition of these attributes, the Apostle writes to us that if we speak in the tongues of men and of angels, but have not love, we are as a resounding gong or clanging cymbals. With the gift of prophesy and the ability to fathom all mysteries and all knowledge, with a faith that can move mountains, yet without love, we are nothing at all.

We may give all we have to the poor and surrender our bodies to the flames; we gain absolutely nothing without love.

The reader would notice that my presentation of this case is very rich in the espousing of love right through; only because of my lifelong experience of God and especially in His Counsel to me over the years.

Love has brought me all I need and far much more; and I know beyond any doubts that the Love of God manifested in Jesus Christ alone holds the Power to avail all goodness, mercies, blessings, grace etc. unto mankind. Only Jesus Christ can save. Nothing in life that we lust after, desire etc. can transform our lives towards Godliness and Holiness unto Eternal Life – to know Jesus Christ, Son of God; and the Power of His Resurrection (Philippians 9:10-11). Jesus Christ was Sent unto mankind for the sole purpose of reconciling us to God unto salvation of our souls. Amen.

The words of 1 Corinthians 13:4-8 are effectively as below:

Love is patient and love is kind. Love does not envy nor boast; and is not proud, rude, self-seeking, easily angered etc. Love keeps no records of wrongs, does not delight in evil but rejoices with good/truth. Love always protects, trusts, hopes and perseveres. Love never fails.

My dear reader, sin is so sweet and very desirable; very attractive, very nice and well presented; and mostly excellently packaged. Sometimes sin is not so sweet, but yet very delicate, always tempting to the senses and lusciously inviting, full of lust etc. Sometimes sin is rather harsh, with false pretensions; nevertheless, to appeal to the human sinful nature to want to achieve, "feel good" (factor) etc; satan presents sin to us in a generally tempting way. Look at a fine example in Proverbs 1 and 2 for starters.

Know this for sure, love is not a feeling, as sin would want you to believe, in the most cunning sense. Love is a choice, a decision, not a feeling at all. The Bible says that the heart is deceitful and desperately wicked (Jeremiah 17:9). Who can know it? Naturally, feelings are heart-led. Yet, even the most learned, even those learned in the Holy Scriptures say things like, follow your heart etc. when asked for counsel or advice. This is a great deception too, absolutely contrary to the Word of God.

God is a Spirit and all those who worship Him must do so in spirit and in truth. As many as are led by the Spirit (Holy) of God are the sons of the Living God. The Bible says not to assess or judge any man any longer after the flesh (1 Corinthians 5:16) but by the spirit. So, if you are feelings-led, you are bound unto errors/falsehoods of/in judgement(s). For, the very perverse, sinful nature wars against the spirit constantly, as the spirit nature against the flesh (Galatians 5:16-17).

Flesh never wants to do the bidding of God Almighty. When we are not fully yielded to Jesus Christ, we are full with lustful wants and desires and readily willing to do the bidding of the flesh as opposed to that of the spirit. This is why we need to have a renewal of our minds and follow after the Standards of God only.

From our available resources, love covers a multitude of sins; and answers all questions. Love covers all and is all in all. Hence, I will go on to elaborate as succinctly as I possibly can on the attributes of love, just for you my reader, to be even more equipped to conquer sin and overcome all hindrances and come to the knowledge of all truth. Come to the River of Life (and of all delight) and drink, buy even milk without money and honey too (Isaiah 55:1). Come and taste and see that indeed, truly, the Lord is Good and His Mercies endure forevermore (Psalm 34:8, 136). Amen.

Come one and come all who are weak and are heavily burdened, let Love give you rest (Matthew 11:28-30). Come all you who are hearing His Voice thorough these words (written/typed with my hands) in this message, come in His Holy Name and let Him show unto you what true love really is all about – a life-changing, transforming, renewing, experience. Come, for all time and in God's Name, Jesus Christ our Lord and Saviour. Amen.

Of Love's Attributes and Aspects...

1. Love is Patient

Well this is very aptly rendered really. It speaks for itself that love is patient. God is said to be slow to anger and abounding in love in the Holy Scriptures (Exodus 34:6; Joel 2:13). Patience is a great virtue.

Imagine that so many things have gone very badly wrong in the affairs of mankind that could have been averted, if only the decisions had been patiently considered, rather than speedily taken. Today we live in a microwave and internet world. Super highways and fast-tracking for various aspects of life including for food and information processing, is the order of the day.

Are you patient? If not, submit to God/Love. Take time to humble yourself totally; and learn to practice love in giving and receiving. Practice to be patient. This would reduce unnecessary anxiety(ies) in your life and I assure you of a better quality of life, even in Christ Jesus, which is my primary concern in this message. Some can give but are unable to receive. Others receive but cannot give. With God's Help, you can learn to give and receive love; knowing of course that it is always better to give than to receive (Acts 20:35).

Do not be surprised that as you put love to good nurturing and effective application in your life daily, even your health (physical, mental and all) will begin to receive positive regeneration.

The overcoming of various anxieties in your life will begin to allow healing to flow into other areas that anxiety for instance has affected and you will know the difference for good. As you increase in patience, your relationships will change for the better. Life is no bed of roses; but generally, you will have much more peace in your life with the increase of patience in your life. Jesus Christ said to cast our cares upon Him (Psalm 55:22; 1 Peter 5:7).

Patience will give the nearest option to you, when you want less anxieties and troubles in your life. Especially with Jesus having made you such an offer to be anxious over nothing (Philippians 4:6) but in everything through prayer and thanksgiving to submit to God in Christ Jesus and let your lives be enriched with the Love of God.

As you obey Love and put patience to practice, love will begin to take root in your life in a deeper sense. Your sense of appreciation of God and why you are here on earth will increase and you will be more sensitive to Life, even Jesus Christ. You will surely begin to receive the strength to fear God more and learn more of the other attributes of love and be more patient to put them to practice.

Patience will help put your new learning to better and more effective use in day to day application. This will manifest in more positive thoughts, words, deeds; and generally, in good works, in Jesus' Name. Amen. Patience is a crucial part of love and with patience, all things will become more meaningful to you. Imagine walking through a park or along a beach with patience and in peace. What a change that would bring. You can appreciate even nature, far better.

2. Love is Kind

Love is full of kindness in thoughts, words and deeds. So, are you kind? If you are, continue and keep on increasing in your kindness for in due season you will reap a bountiful harvest. If not, you must now change your ways consciously.

Begin to check yourself at your points/areas of unkindness and make a conscious decision/choice to be kindly in your daily disposition in every area of your life. You can learn to be kind and kindly disposed by seeking for God's Help and actually doing something practically, to make that change happen. You will surely be duly rewarded.

This will work for you as the Biblical Balm of Gilead (Jeremiah 8:22), to sooth and calm every area of your life. Kindness when combined with patience will promote light in your life and even your heart will be free from the guilt of life. You will make more sense to others in your life and your relationships will be more fruitful and your self-confidence will grow. People will be more kindly disposed to you as you do likewise.

Even your enemies will notice. The Word of God says that if a man's ways are pleasing to the Lord God Almighty, even his enemies will want to be his friend (Proverbs 16:7) and come and bow down before him (Isaiah 60:14). The Holy Spirit of God will begin to notice you (Psalm 34:7) and you will be able to think even deeper and this will draw you to meditate more on God and God will draw closer to you. Do not rest on your oars though; for the journey of love is not one that ends. Love is eternal. So, continue to practice all the attributes and you will find that they all link into one another and work together for the mutual good of all. Do not give up.

3. Love does not envy

Yes, love is not jealous. God reserves the right to be jealous for Himself alone. How many relationships, marriages, friendships etc. have come to ruin because of the "green-eyed monster" as some people call it? How many never see the light of day likewise? Jealousy is sinful and full with evil. Jealousy does not forgive easily at all. Even husbands and wives get attacked with jealousy and they brutalise and destroy each other. Why

169

not rather be wrong(ed) and let God take Glory (1 Corinthians 6:7)? You do not have to suffer divorce because of having been cheated if you will allow forgiveness.

I know this is easier for women who have been cheated as the nature of life is such that when a man has other women, not all is ruined as per profanity of the procreative ability of mankind. God's order looks kindly upon man with more than one wife, as evident in the Word of God.

However, when a woman has other men, paternity is jeopardised. This is frowned upon mostly and this is more grievous evil, even unto God. I speak only of the Wisdom of God here. Only the mature in spirit will understand the mind of God in this matter. However, It is better to be faithful; for God recommends one man one wife (1 Corinthians 7:2) and hates divorce (Malachi 2:16).

To envy is to be dissatisfied with what you have and focused externally on what others have. Envy leads one to assume that these others are better than you; and that you are perhaps not good enough. You assume that because they have what you do not have or have taken an interest in your spouse etc. (which is sometimes not the case at all; for not all that glitters is gold, not everything that we see is for real), as such you end up very envious/jealous. It can go either way; i.e. you covet in envy or wallow in envy due to jealousy.

Coveting is basically rooted in jealousy (we shall come to this later). Many go as far as to hurt others and damage their possessions and or defile their possessions as they feel at the time because of envy/jealousy. God is not pleased with this sin at all. It is wicked. God hates such behaviour; so judge yourself correctly according to love and relevant aspects of love. Rebuke satan in your life. Resist the devil and he will flee (James 4:7).

Do your best to change and modify your behaviour in accordance with God's Word. Stop being envious/jealous of others. Pray for strength to resist this evil and you will overcome in Jesus' Name. If you believe and submit your will to God and strongly desire change, God Will Help you in Jesus' Name. Call on Him, ask God for Help. Do not be prideful and let satan have his way in your life. Allow for God's Love in the Name of Jesus Christ. You will begin to see a positive change in your every thought, word and deed/action. Your destiny will take a newer, healthier path.

4. Love does not boast

Love is not about being overbearingly boisterous with what one has or has achieved to the point of insecurity in oneself and in others. To loudly acclaim oneself for public or private "show off" is considered a hindrance in love. It only espouses feelings of insecurity, inferiority, immaturity etc.; wanting to prove that one is worth something or has achieved something, doing some good, etc., and wanting the whole world to know.

The Word of God tells us that the left hand should not know what the right hand is doing (Matthew 6:3) when giving for example. So, If you are guilty, knowing you are "show-offs" (male and female), boastful etc., give it all up; so Jesus can take Glory. Let Jesus Christ take control of your lives and do not be so egocentric (self focused). If willingly obedient and sincere, God Will Help you to renew your mind in the Name of Jesus Christ, Amen.

5. Love is not proud

Pride begets a fall (Proverbs 16:18). It is said that pride goes before a fall; even as humility begets grace. Grace attends much humility. Humility is the opposite of pride and begets/precedes much Grace. To be haughty, arrogant and look down on others is prideful and sinful. God hates this. God opposes the proud and gives Grace to the humble (James 4:6; 1 Peter 5:5-6). To exalt oneself in one's mind and heart at the expense of all else around one, is sinful and ungodly.

It is very easy to fall under the pride-induced life anywhere. So, the student of love, the follower of Jesus Christ must learn to be humble with God and man. Then God promises to lift us up when we humble ourselves before Him. Moses was said to be the meekest, most humble man (Numbers 12:13) who ever lived. Our Lord Jesus Christ was meek and humble in disposition being in very nature and essence, God.

So, seek after humility and quit being prideful in spirit, soul, body, thoughts, words and deeds. God will uplift and reward humility with much Grace and Divine Favour. Put this to practice and watch love increase in your life, unfailingly.

6. Love is not rude

Beloved, rudeness stinks really. To be disrespectful in thoughts words and deeds is abominably obnoxious. Rudeness in essence emanates from a heart that is impure, hardened, angry and probably possessed, as a result of persistence in evil/idolatry. Rudeness displays ill manners in every way – temperament and all.

Rudeness says all the time, more or less, that it is all about me and if you do not like it, tough. To be rude is to be impolite. So, if you know that you are impolite, abusive, disrespectful, careless for others' and or their feelings, concerns etc., then you can choose to change and become polite, respectful, careful, sensitive to others' feelings, concerns etc. You can choose to not mistreat others anymore and continuously check yourself and your behaviour/attitude to others.

A lot of love's attributes are achievable if we determine to love, choose love, choose to be loving and kindly in disposition. Then God's Hand Will be free to Help us as we invite Him through our obedience to love's call to change and allow our minds to be renewed. Amen, in Jesus' Name.

7. Love is not selfish (self-seeking)

Many of love's attributes (indeed all) are overlapping. Selfish, self-seeking, self-centredness can lead to and or result from pride, unkindness, etc. To want and cater only for oneself is wrong, sinful, ungodly and unloving. To put others before oneself is what love recommends. God first of course and self, last. However, our world today tells us otherwise and looking after "number one" (self) is the bane of today's society.

So, the followers of Jesus Christ will have to swim against the tides, which is a sacrifice, a disciplined exercise, but profitable unto God for Eternal Life in Christ Jesus. Amen. Selfishness causes one to be greedy with any and everything. Wanting the best at the expense of all, regardless of any circumstances that may warrant caution and or sharing. Selfishness wants the biggest share and lusts for more.

So, to increase in love is to quit being selfish and embrace a giving nature. The Bible says it is better to give than to receive. Then God is Exalted and love promoted. God Will Bless the sacrifice of love in giving of oneself and or one's property(ies), resources, selflessly. Amen, in Jesus' Name, to anyone who will follow through with obedience to become unselfish in life's journey.

8. Love is not easily angered

Oh what sins have been committed out of sheer anger, leading unto fiery outbursts of temperaments against loved ones, enemies etc. God tells us in His Word, that in our anger, we must not sin (Ephesians 4:26). Anger hardly ever bears good fruits; rather, it mostly bears evil fruits, because satan capitalises on it. Hence, love exercises restraint continuously from anger.

Anyone who is willing for the sake of God's Love to control his/her temper and forsake anger and the sin potential of it is in line for great Blessings. Patience comes into play here very much indeed. God Will honour such a person. This leads me to the next attribute (also related). So desist from anger and in your anger if ever angry, refrain from sin.

9. Love is long-suffering

Love bears up with Godly countenance under much pain, suffering and injustice. This takes much patience too; and kindly disposition. Instead of giving in to anger, under such conditions as mentioned (diverse sufferings), love bears up with much fortitude, under the weight of injustices, pain etc. This is a most valuable aspect of love. For the Bible tells us that anyone who truly wants to and follows Jesus Christ and wants to live a Godly life in Jesus Christ will face persecution (2 Timothy 3:12).

So, we must go through much suffering and pain as part of our process of purification, sanctification, maturing unto the image and likeness of Jesus Christ, our Lord and Saviour, even unto His likeness and character. Such long-suffering is accounted unto the true believer as pleasing unto God in Jesus Christ (Romans 8:17-18; Matthew 5:1-11).

So, beloved, be very patient and persevere in doing good, even and especially under the weight of injustice (James 1:12) etc. God Will Bless anyone who would put these attributes to practice day to day in Jesus' Name. Amen.

10. Love keeps no records of wrongs

Forgiveness is essential in love. The Bible says do not let the sun go down when you are still angry (i.e. having taken offence); deal with all such matters quickly. In not keeping a record of wrongdoings against us, we learn to forgive, even as we are forgiven by God. We learn to forget too; as God forgets even our own worst sins against Him when we seek for His forgiveness and choose to live for Him. Many have become sick and even died from anxieties and cares/worries of life. This links up with love not being easily angered. When you keep no records of wrongdoing, you control your anger indirectly, which is profitable in love.

Unforgiveness is a principal culprit in wrecking lives. To be in love's light, we must learn to forgive and allow God to avenge sins against us. Vengeance is Mine says the Lord, I will repay (Romans 12:19). We are urged by the Word of God in Jesus Christ even to forgive our enemies in saying that we should love our enemies. If we can love our enemies, it cannot be difficult to forgive those who are not our enemies. When we do this then we really truly show that we are followers of Jesus Christ. Yet, many of us find forgiving so hard and difficult like a taboo.

So, you who never forgives/forgets; nor do you let anyone get away with sinning against you (no matter who or what they have done to you). Give it all up to Jesus Christ. Forgive and forget even as you seek for God's Favour to forgive you your sins and cast them into the sea of forgetfulness. God is kind and merciful to you; so, be kindly and merciful too, putting this into practice. Then, God's love will surely increase in your life and you will be as a new man, increasingly empowered by the Holy Spirit to overcome all evil as you practice faith that works through love in Jesus Christ's Holy Name. Amen.

11. Love does not delight in evil but rejoices with the Truth

Love hates evil; loves and embraces the Truth. A heart that always loves is saddened by evil and is uncomfortable with evil and doers of evil. However, the opposite is the case with love when it comes to Truth and the lovers of Truth. Then love rejoices and is heartened with enthusiasm generated by joy.

So, you who is steeped in evil, get out from amongst your fellow evil doers. Begin to love and embrace the Truth and rejoice accordingly. Flee from evil and avoid all appearances of evil (1 Thessalonians 5:22). Resist the devil and he will flee from you. This will please our Father in Heaven and Jesus Christ Will Pour out His Holy Spirit upon all who put to practice the love of Truth. Amen.

12. Love always protects, trusts, hopes and perseveres

Love always protects. Love will not cast one another to the dogs. Love instinctively wants to build, protect, rather than destroy. Although God who is Love destroys evil, He is Gracious; abounding in love and full of mercy.

Love always hopes and will not ever give up. Love always trusts in God's love and promises, which are yes and amen in Christ Jesus (2 Corinthians 1:20). Amen. Love trusts in others too, regardless of having been hurt etc. Love always gives a chance to others to rebuild trust. Love always perseveres and never gives up on the practice of love and hospitality (Romans 12:13), especially unto the household of believers. Love goes all the way and will even go the extra mile or two.

Love always honours God. The combination of love's various attributes and aspects lead up to Eternal Life for it builds anyone up unto perfection and holiness in thoughts, words and deeds and unto/for all eternity. Love continues in doing good, supporting good, truth and righteousness. Can you check yourself and see where you are wanting for love? Where are you lacking? Will you dare to put love to practice daily until love becomes a part of you, then you will have a change of life and God will be pleased with you.

13. Love never fails

This is so very succinct. Love is forever and will not fail to yield good fruits. How love is abused daily though, for our lack of respect nor honour for God. If people come to the understanding of true love, there will be more honour for God (Love). Love is endless. Love always succeeds. Let no one deceive you that love ends. Love never ends.

Love is so awesome. Let all who want for love begin to let the light of love search their hearts, minds, souls, bodies, beings etc. and open up all that is not of God (i.e. contrary to love). If anyone will willingly let go of all that is darkness, contrary to love, in their lives and receive love's many attributes in the place of all that is contrary, such people will surely be transformed for good.

Let such a person begin today not tomorrow to submit all evil (anti-love) attitudes, behaviours, thoughts, words, deeds etc. Let them begin to practice love with the fear of God and look to the eternal hope, even through Jesus Christ our Lord God. Then be ready and willing to receive from God, abundant light with much grace and Blessings in Jesus Christ. Amen.

Take the Mask Off...

Now I hear the Voice of my Lord's Holy Spirit telling me that no one will be rejected by Him, when such a person is willing to do all it takes to give up on all evil and all idolatry (Amos 5:15; Micah 7:18; Zephaniah 3:13; Romans 11:5). Even if you do not have the will/strength, but you are sincerely willing, the Lord Shall come to your aid in Jesus' Name. The words I have written in this book are not mine; they are Living Oracles of the Lord Jesus Christ, Himself, the Word of God. To Him be all Praise, Honour, Glory and Adoration, for ever and ever, Amen.

How long will you allow satan to have you "on-side", to inflict havoc on other humans, your fellow human beings, etc.? Do you profess Christianity and know within yourself that you are not a Christian? You discriminate against the poor and needy (James 2:3-5). You have no mercy. You engage in "eye service" (only when you are being watched are you faithful etc.) and please only those who are valuable to/for you or those close to you. You practice favouritism freely. You withhold good from people unjustly, when it is within your power to act (Proverbs 3:27).

You who remain in the occult and say that you were sent in there to make changes by God Almighty. You not only practice homosexuality, lesbianism, adultery, sorcery, paganism and various idolatries, you promote the practice of them even publicly.

You remain a satanist, witch, wizard etc., yet remain in the so-called churches as the most or one of the most active members (Romans 1, note verse 32).

You cheat and beat up on your husband/wife and irrationally wallop your children and or deny them love. The Word of God says not to exasperate your children (Ephesians 6:4). You have held your husband bound and he is now like your wife; this for no unjust cause. You have held your wife bound likewise and you are always in church (Ephesians 5:22-33)?

You claim to call on the name of God and you use your children as slaves, even sexually. You do the same with your wife and your husband. You treat your workers with disdain and deny them their wages when due (Leviticus 19:13; Deuteronomy 24:15; Malachi 3:5; Luke 10:7). You practice racism, tribalism and the likes.

You have by this disallowed many from being fulfilled in their lives. You have thus helped some people to an early grave (Ezekiel 13:19). Because of you, some have committed suicide. You say you are a child and for reasons of indiscipline, you eat up your parents' members; and pledge your co-siblings for game in your evil meetings. You look at your loved ones and others alike with the evil eye. You sincerely believe all is hidden. Does not God see you (Luke 8:17, 12:2)? Is not Jesus Christ the Judge Standing at the door?

Mr, Mrs, Ms Apostle, Prophet, Evangelist, Pastor and Teacher, who are you fooling? Are you following God's Word or your own rebellious heart? With your seductive charms (Ezekiel 13:18-20) and all, ruining households (Titus 1:11), who called you? God? Or man? Well, the Judge is Standing at the door.

Mr, Mrs, Ms President, Prime Minister, King, Queen, Head of State etc., How about all the blood you have shed to get to where you are; the defrauding of your nation; raping of other nations in the world; your love for oil, power and the occult etc. (Proverbs 29:2, 12)? You can call on God all the time as you do in whatever way you like. You cannot hide from the only true God of Abraham, Isaac and Jacob, who is called Israel.

What about all the rings and chains (neck and hand) you use like amulets on your arms, ankles, necks, fingers, toes etc., even on your waist? In your head dress, in your (wo)manhood etc. to ensnare and bewitch? Does not God see you? The incisions you have procured – under your tongues and around your body and on your head have been seen by God (Isaiah 3).

You want to wave your hand and have people fall under the "power of God"? You now take God's Power for a show and mess up the lives of many young ones too. You bewitch and drain members of your congregation freely and leave the sick unattended and cause the healthy to be sick (Zechariah 11:15-17).

You may fool some of the people some of the time, be assured that you cannot fool all of the people all of the time. Surely you cannot fool God. Does not God and His True servants see through your mask? You are a masquerade only onto yourself and those who sold their souls to you. Who called you? Do I know you? No wonder the fear of God is not in you.

You hate to teach the fear of God to others. Rather, you teach others not to fear me, the God of Israel. Rather, they fear you. Alas. I will show you very soon that I am the God of Abraham, Isaac and Jacob (Israel). I will repay you for your evil. I will arise and cause your charms etc. etc. to become an abomination onto you; even as you have desecrated my holy temple, so will you be desecrated wherever you go. I will dishonour you. Your power will become nothingness. Your gold and silver will become corroded (James 5:3). They will burn your skin. I will cause you grief.

You allow the free reign of sexual perversions and immorality and not only do you yourselves wear the adulterous and seductive looks, you condone it in your assemblies which you present to the world in my Name. You teach your ways to your children too and destroy many young ones, totally oblivious of my Word against such behaviour and my ability to punish severely for such (Matthew

18:6, 10, 14). You have allowed jezebel, feminism and political correctness and all such evil in my Name (Revelations 2:20; 1 Kings 21:23)? Should I be pleased with you for these?

You allow free reign of evil in places you call church where I cannot bear to stand in. How can I be in your evil assemblies (Isaiah 1:12-14)? You debase and destroy your young ones even before they know what they are doing. Is not this a sacrificing of these young ones unto molech (Leviticus 18:21; Jeremiah 32:35)? Because you are so stubborn, arrogant and out of control, satan and his cohorts are made so comfortable and welcome amongst you and in your gatherings.

You look, talk, dress, act, think, speak and carry on in life as you like; rather than seek for my Counsel. You say the Lord does not care about such things. You call up and embrace all and sundry, including the most wicked, for their money. You place them in positions of authority, to care for and watch over my Word and my flocks. The fear of God is far from you as my Spirit is far from you.

For satanic powers to control and ruin the lives of others, you rape and murder children, women, the elderly, the poor, aliens, etc. just to satisfy satan. You covet your neighbours' wife and defile his daughters too. You covet her husband and defile her sons too. You have sex with animals as well as men having sex with men and women with women and horrendous acts against your body.

You drink human and animal blood and eat human flesh as meat too. You deny the aliens living amongst you justice and cause their cries to come up to me (Malachi 3:5; Luke 18:7). You behave as though I am far away and cannot see. Therefore, unless you repent, I shall arise with renewed vigour and act. Then, you will know that I am the LORD. I do not change and will never share my Glory with any man.

181

Well, as you are full of evil, I have news for you. God is nearer than you could ever imagine. You have misjudged your creator. Yet, if you will acknowledge your guilt, confess and repent of your sins and expose satan; if you will come running to God in Jesus Christ, I will yet forgive you and snatch you from the fire. No matter the depth your sins. No matter how deep in sin you are, do not give up hope; for, in Jesus Christ, there is the offer of forgiveness of sins and so repent and open your heart today (2 Chronicles 7:14; 1 Peter 5:6).

Confess your sins and receive Godly Counsel. If no one will hear you nearby, write to my servant (the writer/deliverer of this message). Hide nothing for satan will use whatever you do not confess against you at an opportune time. God will Touch you and change your heart if you are willing and obedient. Your life will be redeemed through the Blood of Jesus Christ. Be bold and courageous.

You have done much and endured much for satan; and for what does not profit or last, you have forsaken my love. Will it now be too much for you to give all up and enter into the Love of your Creator that will give you life, even eternal life in Jesus Christ? This will last forever. You have a choice of a new life now will you yield? Or will you rather go with satan, your lover till Judgment Day? The choice is entirely yours. The Lord has Spoken.

Okay, you. How about you who are bound up in all kinds of evil, dominions, powers of darkness and in sin. You engage in so much darkness that light scares you. You masquerade yourself in so much falsehood, make-up, etc. and go out of your way to make yourself look so "good". Do you know the meaning of "good"? You desecrate all that is good in you and make yourself look even worse than the "prostitute" who hates her/his life.

You make a mockery of God before sinners, by living their lives and pretending to be a child of God. I will expose you and your nakedness will be seen henceforth. I will strip you of all your powers and your wealth will be plundered. You have seduced your way to the top of the worldly domains and dominions using my Name in vain. You want to possess the media so you can be famous like the human "stars". You feign humility and fool many. Not me. Watch, if you do not change, I will expose you.

The kings and queens of the red light and other evil domains laugh at you, even as you claim to be children of God. So you think because you are not known publicly for what you do secretly, you think you will get away? I will expose you. You are worse than those who publicly engage in their evil for all to see. Your guilt is superior because you use My Name says the Lord. They do not see you at night when you relieve yourself of the evil you have polluted yourself with during the day and in the morning when you have polluted yourself in the night.

You make a show of your so-called good deeds. You do not fool me. I am your maker and know your heart. I see you. You are not clean inside, because you feign holiness. Because you are not known or seen by the world does not mean that you are of God. I tell you that you will be more severely punished for you do all you do and claim that you are born again in Jesus Christ. You think your are okay, because the people of the world always pretend to believe you. You think that they do not know you?

You fool only yourself. The worldly ones know those of the world and it is because you are of the world that they are comfortable with you and pretending with you. They made the masks that you wear. Remember this. Moreover, that is why you are so empty inside for you cannot be clean when you live a lie before Almighty God.

I am coming soon (Revelation 22:12, 20). You have been warned over and over again. If you do not repent, it will be too late (Revelation 1-3). On that day there will be no mercy. Because God is slow to anger and abounding in Love does not make God a weak God. I will yet show to you that I am the Living God in Christ Jesus.

Jehovah is my Name. I am the I AM. Do you not remember me from of old? I am the Lord and I change not.

Come now, do not delay, I will do all I promised to do (Joshua 21:45; Psalm 119:140; 2 Corinthians 1:20). Come today and save yourself from the impending doom; then, maybe you may save some of your hearers. Jesus Christ will set you free. There is yet hope for you as long as there is still daylight. Come all you who labour and are heavily laden/burdened. Come all you that are weary. Jesus Christ will give you rest. Dare to believe, be bold.

So your family and friends etc. may/will not approve? Well, if you are ashamed of me, then I will be ashamed of you before my Father (Luke 9:26). It is after all your life and you do have the choice to do with it as you please. Continue (if you choose) to seek/crave after man's approval/applause or let God in Jesus Christ purge you and refine you and save you from eternal damnation.

Oh okay, everything is going very well for you? Fine. Business is good. Also, you who have turned my house into a den of robbers, I am here. You are even married (with or without a bit on the side). Well done. You are well known as a pious godly person but you know what you do when no one is watching.

But I tell you; I am watching over all, to fulfil my Word (Revelation 17:17), even in Christ Jesus. Amen. Your generosity and faithfulness to the church you call your church will not save you from eternal damnation. The one whom you readily mask away from you and deceive, Jesus Christ is His Name. He alone can save. Again I tell you, only Jesus Can Save. Jesus Christ is the Great Judge.

Repent whilst there is yet HOPE...

The Judge is Standing at the door (James 5:8-10). He is now calling to you. Come O sinner and repent of your ways. Seek for forgiveness and receive pardon. Let Me make your life worthwhile. Let me renew and refresh your soul. I will cause you to be a new person if you will heed this warning. Tomorrow may be too late. You may never get another chance again. Let Jesus Christ be Lord and Saviour over your life so you can have life at the end of this sojourn on earth. Do not harden your heart (Hebrew 4:6-8).

There will be no more mercy when the Time comes on that Day. The Day of the Lord is going to be a terrible, dreadful day (Joel 2:10-12, 30-32). Shame? Ashamed? No do not be; for this profits nothing unto you at this time. This is a time when the Victory Train (Psalm 68:18; Ephesians 4:8) is stopping and picking up the beloved of the Lord. Now is the time of salvation. Today is your day for salvation. The coming of Jesus Christ is very near (Revelation 22:7, 12, 20).

This writer is only a small part of this preparation. However, the love of God compels me to call you my reader unto faith, love in holiness. The revival is very near you. The Lord of the Revival is waiting on you right now.

Do not allow your love of this world to deprive you of Eternal Life through and **only in** Jesus Christ. Do not love the world or anything that is in the world (James 4:1-10; 1 John 2:15-17). Do you not know that the Love of the Father in Jesus Christ cannot abide within anyone who loves the world? The love of the world is like friendship with the world. This is enmity towards God Almighty. For everything in this wicked world, the cravings of sinful man, lust of the eyes, the sweetness of sin and boastfulness regarding your possessions and or achievements are of the world and not from God.

All men are like grass (1 Peter 1:24-25) and all their glory, like the flowers of the fields – which wither and fall respectively. However, the Word of the Lord Stands forevermore in Jesus Christ our Lord. Amen. Give up on worldly lusts (Proverbs 28:13). The "helping" God to make you look "beautiful" etc. are of the world, not of God. Even so, all your masking will never and has never satisfied you anyway. It only attracts you unto more sin and lusts from others etc. and you can pretend all you want but you are causing the fall of many (1 Corinthians 8:13). For this you will give an account.

The vacuum you try to fill and or cover up with all the make up and masking remains nevertheless; for only Jesus Christ can save you. Honour the temple. Honour the Lord of the Temple (1 Corinthians 6:20; 1 Peter 4:1). I could go on and on forever, it is now left with you my reader. You now have no further excuses (John 15:22; Romans 1:20).

If you know that you are in Jesus Christ, I particularly encourage you to persevere (Jude 1; James 1:12, 5:11; Hebrews 10:35-37) in faithfulness, doing good and working through love. Stand for Jesus Christ in the face of what is around now and what is to come; for a great testing is just around the corner and it will be very easy, even for the elect if it were possible, to be deceived. So, stand firm lest you fall (1 Corinthians 10:12; Mark 13:13).

Stand, even in the face of death, for Jesus Christ. Stand, even unto death. Do not allow anyone to discourage (Joshua 1:8-10) you. Guard your spirit. Pray ceaselessly. Despise not prophesying. Hold onto the good (1 Thessalonians 5:16-18). Be bold and of good cheer.

Let the LIGHT and love and beauty of the LORD Jesus Christ be seen in you always (1 Peter 3:1-6). Continue to meditate upon the Word of God (Psalm 119:22-28, 98-99). Do not allow the Law (the Word of God in Spirit and Truth) to depart from your mouth and your heart. Meditate day and night on the Word of God. Do and observe what is written (James 1:22-23; 1 John 2:4;) to be fully obedient to God's Word. Practice, obedience always. Then you will have good success (Joshua 1:7-8). Let no one deceive you that God's Love is unconditional.

It is a lie. There is nowhere in the Word of God where it says that God's Love is unconditional and for all. God's Love is always with condition (obedience). God requires your obedience and mine. Yes, we are given the will to choose otherwise; but, God's love is not at all automatic (Romans 9:13; Malachi 1:2-3; Psalm 22:37; Proverbs 3:33; Deuteronomy 28). God does not love all equally at all. Even as your fingers are not equal, God chooses whom He Blesses. Many preach this to satisfy itching ears. All through the Holy Scriptures, it is made abundantly clear that Blessings reward obedience and curses reserved for disobedience.

The Word of God will never change to suit or pamper human whims and or caprices (1 Samuel 15:29; James 1:17; Malachi 3:6). Rather, we must pass through the fire of affliction (Isaiah 43:2; James 1:2-12) or whatever it takes to be saved. We must change and be submissive to the Holy Spirit and to God's Word to allow for the renewing of minds to take place. Only then can we have the chance to partake of the Kingdom of God. God is not mocked; we shall all reap whatsoever we sow.

By all means, judge yourself, lest you be Judged (Matthew 7:1). Judgement ultimately shall begin in the Church with the Elders (Ezekiel 9:6; Isaiah 3:14;). But all shall face Judgement (Ecclesiastes 3:17, 11:9; Romans 14:10). Jesus Christ is the Supreme and Ultimate Judge (John 5:22).

So, you judge yourself continuously and do not be caught napping (Mark 13:33; 1 Peter 5:8). However, the man of God shall be a judge of all things and subjected to no man's judgment (1 Corinthians

2:15). The time is so short as our Lord Jesus Christ's coming draws nearer and nearer.

Better be prepared in and out of season (2 Timothy 4:1-3) rather than be sorry. Be safe. Again, if you are standing stand firm so that you do not fall. Only those who stand firm to the very end shall be saved (Mark 13:13; 1 Corinthians 10:12). For you who are weak like me, submit absolutely for God to take up your cause so you may receive Strength in Jesus Christ. Amen.

Take up your cross (Luke 9:23; Matthew 10:38); like me, follow Jesus Christ relentlessly against all odds. With God all things are possible. Only believe. Let nothing separate you from the love of Jesus Christ. When you have been made strong, you of course, must strengthen your brethren.

Romans 8:31 to the end will serve to refresh and encourage you always. Nothing will harm you if you will devote all to Jesus Christ. Nothing must be allowed to separate us from the Love of Jesus Christ. Pray and do not give up. Regardless of what you face, do not give up. Soon, your testimony shall even empower, embolden and strengthen others. I pray in Jesus' Holy Name. Amen.

Additional Exhortations...

Then Jesus came to them (the disciples) and said that all authority in Heaven and on earth has been given to Him (Matthew 28:17-20). Therefore He Commanded them to go and make disciples of all men (in all nations); baptising them in the Name of the Father, Son and Holy Spirit; teaching them to obey everything He had commanded them. Surely, He said to them that He Is with them always to the very end of the age. Amen.

I know that my God through Jesus Christ's Holy Spirit and His Holy Name shall prove Himself in Touching hearts, minds, souls and all (no matter how hard/corrupt) through this message. God is Faithful (Deuteronomy 7:9, 32:4; Romans 3:1-8; 1 Corinthians 10:13). Will you be? Receive the Breath of God right through and right now in Jesus' Name. Amen. Be delivered right through and right now in Jesus' Name. Amen. Thank You Father in Jesus Christ's Holy Name that You always hear me. Amen.

Concluding...

If you have not done so already, I now invite you to do a most sincere soul searching and unload all your concerns and anxieties (Psalm 55:22; 1 Peter 5:7), for Jesus Christ to relieve you for good. You can make a commitment to draw nearer (Hebrews 10:1,22; James 4:8) and nearer forever to God through Jesus Christ. This must be, is and will be your decision, your choice. No one can live for Jesus Christ for another person. A choice has been given to each person, his own decision and his own responsibility.

Be assured, it is not an easy journey to Heaven; and it will never be easy (Matthew 7:13-14). Jesus Christ will honour you and pour out His Holy Spirit unto you (Joel 2:28-29) if you will continuously persevere and not ever give up praying fervently and always being grateful for His Help. You must be born again (John 3).

Feel free to write to me should you be in need of prayers, help, counsel, support or further direction and or guidance. This offer is only for the truly serious. No time wasters please. Time is very short. A gentle word can break a bone (Proverbs 25:15). Many lost souls, hardened by the world have come into the Light of Jesus Christ, saved from false idols, religions, teachings, and lives. So, be bold. Do take the mask(s) off. May God in Jesus Christ Help you as you do so. Amen.

BEHOLD...... THE FLAMING SWORD!
HE IS THE WORD OF GOD; JESUS CHRIST IS HIS NAME
HE IS THE LORD GOD ALMIGHTY. AMEN.

Prophet Folayan Osekita MBA
windowsofheavenoutreach@yahoo.co.uk
www.windowsofheaven.co.uk